Zen Meditation
plain and
simple

by Albert Low

Tuttle Publishing
Boston • Rutland, Vermont • Tokyo

First published in 1989 as *An Invitation to Practice Zen* by Tuttle
Publishing, an imprint of Periplus Editions (HK) Ltd, with editorial
offices at 153 Milk Street, Boston, Massachusetts 02109.

Library of Congress Catalog Card Number: 89-50020
ISBN: 0-8048-3211-0

Distributed by

USA
Tuttle Publishing
Distribution Center
Airport Industrial Park
364 Innovation Drive
North Clarendon, VT 05759-9436
Tel: (802) 773-8930
Tel: (800) 526-2778

JAPAN
Tuttle Publishing
RK Building, 2nd Floor
2-13-10 Shimo-Meguro, Meguro-Ku
Tokyo 153 0064
Tel: (03) 5437-0171
Fax: (03) 5437-0755

CANADA
Raincoast Books
8680 Cambie Street
Vancouver, British Columbia
V6P 6M9
Tel: (604) 323-7100
Fax: (604) 323-2600

SOUTHEAST ASIA
Berkeley Books Pte Ltd
5 Little Road #08-01
Singapore 536983
Tel: (65) 280-1330
Fax: (65) 280-6290

First edition, 1989
Twelfth printing, 2000

Printed in the United States of America

TO
Anita, John, and Steve

Contents

Contents

Acknowledgments

I should like to acknowledge the help that I received from the Montreal Zen community, many of whom have read and commented upon the text. In particular I should like to thank Alan Travers, Tony Stern, and Ovid Avarmaa for their comments and suggestions, and to Toufik Moussa, who drew the illustrations. Grateful acknowledgment is also extended to the Rochester Zen Center for permission to quote its versions of *The Prajna Paramita Hridaya Sutra*, *Hakuin Zenji's Chant in Praise of Zazen*, the *Ten-Verse Kannon Sutra*, and *The Four Vows*.

I should also like to thank my wife, Jean, for her unfailing support.

Introduction

The introduction of a book is usually used by its author to tell the reader what the book is about in a very general way. This gives an overview of the book and sets the reader going in the right direction. In the introduction the author says, in effect, this is what I am trying to accomplish by writing this book. However, instead of simply doing this, I should like to ask you, the reader, to join in and do some of the work of the introduction with me.

This book is about Zen and is intended for people who know little or nothing about the subject. To this end the presentation has been simplified as much as possible so that the reader can see the whole wood and not get hung up on one or another tree. Zen is essentially a practice and not a theory or dogma. Later, if you persevere, finer points will arise that will become clarified as you go on, but in a natural, intuitive way.

Now I would like you to ask yourself a question, and I'll give some help to you in answering: "Why should *I* be interested in a book on the practice of Zen?" Please think about your answer as you read the rest of this introduction; in this way you should get a much better orientation about the book than one that comes from the author alone, and this will make the book much more vital to you, much more alive.

First of all, have you come to this book simply out of curiosity? Were you browsing among the books in a bookshop and just happened to pick up this particular book and are now glancing through it? Or have you heard a little about Zen from a friend, or from a TV program, and are curious to know more about it? Curiosity is a strange thing. We always seem to want to know more; we are always wondering, examining, studying. This is not only true of human beings; all living things seem to be imbued with curiosity. Have you ever watched a kitten and noticed how it will inspect everything—smelling, patting, biting, ever interested to know more? The word "curious" has family connections with two other words: "care" and "cure." It is understandable that a cat would be careful and would want to know what sort of things are around. The family connection between curious and care is therefore obvious. But why the connection with cure? What is curiosity a cure for?

Perhaps it is not curiosity that prompts you to be interested in an introduction to Zen. Perhaps you are among those who are looking for physical well-being. We are probably living in the most health-conscious age ever, and, since our average life expectancy is now about seventy-four, this is with good reason. Is this what you want? Good physical health? Or are you looking for psychological health? Ours is also a "psychological society"; we can now get counseling for almost everything: insomnia, impotence, alcoholism, drug abuse, to improve our relations with others, to gain confidence, and so on. So perhaps you are among the many thousands who would like to practice some form of meditation to help gain physical well-being or mental stability. Many studies have been made showing that high blood pressure can sometimes be controlled, cardiovascular problems ameliorated, and stress-related illness eased with the aid of meditation. Furthermore, many psychotherapists are advising meditation to help their patients gain insight and stability.

Many practice meditation because of its obvious benefits in improving concentration. This improvement can come about not only in the area of purely mental endeavor, such as study, but also in athletics and sports. This is evident when it is remembered that Zen is basic to the martial arts of swordsmanship, karate, and archery. Tradition holds that the art of self-defense without using weapons was introduced into China by a Buddhist monk named Bodhidharma. The Shaolin Temple, where he meditated and practiced, is being renovated and has become a shrine for martial-arts devotees. Bodhidharma was also the first Chinese patriarch of Zen, so there is a common heritage shared by Zen and the martial arts. Indeed, a good karate teacher will always insist upon a good grounding in Zen for his students. Those who have good powers of concentration are not only more likely to perform well at the art, but are also more likely to be able to control themselves and not abuse the power they acquire in the development of their martial-arts skills.

Or perhaps you want to be more creative? We truly cannot become more creative by learning about definitions of creativity or even by studying techniques and ways of being creative. Creativity is the life-force in action; all that is alive is essentially creative. The question then becomes how can we be more alive and less inhibited?

So what do you want? Answers to questions, ways to live, peace and contentment? Ponder on this matter a while. Then please ask yourself another question. Is it enough just to want? Or, to put the question slightly differently, is life simply a routine of wanting and satisfying our wants? There are all kinds of wants: we want to own things, experience things, do things, know things;

we want love, attention, happiness, success, fulfillment. If you go to a shopping mall on a Saturday, you will see hundreds of people, and there are thousands and thousands of similar shopping malls, all with hundreds of people, all wanting things, buying things, and then wanting other things. Is this what life is about—deciding which want to satisfy, satisfying it, then moving on to the next want, and so on? Is life simply a process of setting goals—career goals, life goals, financial goals, security goals, health goals—and then striving to reach them?

Ask yourself: what is life, *my* life, really all about? What is it above all that really matters? Just imagine for a moment that you have a fairy godmother—what will you wish for when she offers just one wish? A million dollars? Someone to love who will love you in return? Success in some project? More knowledge or wisdom? When this question is asked sincerely, when one is not easily satisfied with standard answers, clichés, the conditioning of society, the influence of family, friends, TV, or college, a strange truth emerges: *there is something that one desperately wants but it is nothing that can be given a name.* There is a deep ache, so deep that nothing, it seems, can ever satisfy it. It is not the need for immortality nor for the magical, nor for some idyllic dream. What can it be?

It is this indefinable but nevertheless real want

that underlies all our other wants and all of our curiosity. It is this that makes us search through books in the hope that we might somehow get help. It is this ache for something for which we seek a cure. It might well be what has prompted you to pick up this very book.

Zen will not give you answers. It adheres to no philosophy or theology. But it will help you come to your own answer, one which will not consist of words, definitions, or theories, but will be a new way of seeing yourself and the world. To be able to understand this fully, to understand why there *is really no such thing as Zen*, requires some words and some work. Indeed it requires Zen. This book will provide the words if you will provide the work. This is not strictly a fair bargain, because it will take a lot more work than words, and in the end who can say what you will achieve? Perhaps nothing more than you have already, but, who knows, you may have it in an entirely new way.

Note: Foreign terms are not italicized after they are defined or explained.

PART I
Orientation

(*Overleaf*) Calligraphy by Obaku of a saying of Mokuan: *Ningen tada ichi butsu.* "Human beings are all Buddha."

1

What Is Buddhism?

BUDDHA MEANS AWAKENED ONE

It might be best to start with a little history. However, as you will see, this history is not something remote and abstract; on the contrary, it has a direct bearing on the life of each of us. Zen, as most are now aware, is a sect of Buddhism, and to help lay a foundation for what is to come, we must speak about Buddhism first; then, in the next chapter, we shall speak more specifically about Zen.

The word Buddha means Awakened One. It is a Sanskrit word. Sanskrit is an ancient language that has something in common with Latin in that both are now dead languages but both have been kept in use because of religious needs. However, Sanskrit was once a living language and *buddha* was a living word. It meant "awakening," or "coming to" after a faint or concussion, and thus was part of the everyday language, with no special meaning or overtones. Later it came to mean "spiritual awakening," and yet later still it came to refer to a particular person, Siddhartha Gautama.

Attaining spiritual awakening, the goal of Buddhism, is as old as mankind and is a potential everyone has and always has had. To be human means to have this potential. Thus, strictly speaking, Buddhism cannot be confined to a particular culture or area. However, periodically someone attains to very deep awakening and because of this is able to breath new life into existing spiritual teachings. Such a person was Siddhartha Gautama, whom Buddhists refer to as Buddha.

BUDDHISM AND SHAKYAMUNI

Birth and early life. Siddhartha was born in Northern India. His father, according to tradition, was the chief of a tribe called the Shakyas. Later, when Siddhartha became well known as a wise man, people began to call him Shakyamuni; *muni* means "wise man," or perhaps even "saint," and Shakyamuni was therefore the wise man of the Shakya tribe.

It was the custom for astrologers to be consulted when a child was born, and astrologers predicted that Siddhartha would grow up to be either a king or a monk. A monk in those days lived a painful and arduous life. There were no monasteries but simply monks who wandered, either in small groups or alone ("monk" derives from the Greek *monos,* meaning "alone"), seeking spiritual purification through various ascetic practices, sleeping in the open and obtaining food wherever they could by begging or by eating wild fruits, berries, and herbs. Naturally Siddhartha's father wanted to spare his son such tribulations and so did his best to ensure that the boy, and later the man, was shielded from sights and experiences that would cause him to seek a spiritual path. He had palaces built, surrounded by beautiful gardens and filled with luxury, and he had high walls built around the palaces to keep the world out. By this means he hoped to keep his son from any deep thought or concern.

Siddhartha grew up behind these walls contented, enjoying to the full all that this kind of life had to offer. At age twenty-nine he married and had a son of his own.

Four encounters. Shortly after the birth of his son, however, Siddhartha began to grow restive, finding the luxury irksome and the comfort stifling. More and more he felt that the walls were closing him in, holding him prisoner to a way of life whose excess had itself become a source of pain and a reason for seeking escape.

One day he resolved to break out and visit a

nearby town. Accompanied by his charioteer, he went off in his chariot through the palace gates and along the road to the town. He did not reach the town, however, because along the way he had the first of four encounters that were destined to change his life completely. He saw a sick man tottering along the side of the road, emaciated, bent, and feeble. So far Siddhartha had not met with sickness. It had been kept outside the walls of the palace; only the young and well had been allowed inside. Surprised, he called out to his charioteer to stop and then, pointing to the sick man they had just passed, asked about him. "That, sire," said the charioteer, "is a sick man. Sickness is the lot of us all. All that lives, at some time or another, falls sick." To one who had not even thought about sickness, this encounter and this pronouncement were deeply disturbing. Troubled and confused, he ordered the charioteer to turn the chariot around and return to the palace.

Safely inside the palace gates, Siddhartha resumed his former habits and ways until the old anguish of being a prisoner to pleasure reawakened, and with it the urge to escape once more. Again he made a sortie with his charioteer and for the second time he had an encounter. This time the shock was even more profound. He saw an old man. Questioning his charioteer, he received the answer: "That, sire, is an old man. All that lives grows old." Siddhartha was so disturbed he again fled back to the palace. However, not long afterward another attempt was made to escape from the pain of languishing behind high walls. And once again, along the way Siddhartha met something that shattered him. It was a corpse. When he heard, "All, at some time, must die," he again, in anguish, fled to the security of his palace.

Each encounter had bitten more deeply into Siddhartha's mind, and now it seemed to him he could never rest in peace again. Sickness, old age and death, the curse of life and the burden of insecurity, now haunted him. No walls could now keep out these three, no comfort or luxury banish them, no achievement nullify them.

Someone said that religion begins with the cry for help, and now Siddhartha's whole being was crying for help. He left the walled enclosure once again and had his fourth encounter, the one that profoundly and irrevocably changed his life, and in time, the lives of countless millions of others. He met a monk. When he asked about the monk he was told a monk was one who was seeking a way beyond sickness, old age, and death.

Siddhartha resolved then and there to become a monk himself, to seek this way. At night, when his wife and child, friends, and servants, were all soundly sleeping, he slipped out of the house, through the gates of the grounds and into the nearby forest. There he paused long enough to strip off his fine clothes and to cut away his long hair. Then, leaving behind all that he owned and loved, he went deep into the forest to seek answers to the questions boiling inside him, to extract a meaning from what seemed a meaningless life, to find a way out of the cul-de-sac of existence whose end was sickness, old age, and death.

The search. For six years Siddhartha struggled to find peace of mind. He visited teachers and tried all the known ways, employing all the severe and austere practices of the time. He came to live on the most meager ration of food, so little in fact that, suffering from severe malnutrition, he grew so weak his health began to deteriorate and death seemed inevitable. In this emaciated and tormented state a memory came to him of a time when, as a youth of sixteen, he had one day, sitting under a rose-apple tree, experienced a *oneness* that seemed to pervade all things. He had beheld an unseen unity that binds all together in one vast and boundless universe. He had felt, at that time, that he was close to truth, and now, remembering this years later at the extremity of his endurance, he resolved to find again the door that he had walked up to but not through. After taking some nourishment, he resolved to sit beneath a Bo tree and meditate in order to plumb this unity to its depths. He vowed to continue meditating even if his flesh were to dry up and his bones crumble and turn to dust, and not to stop until he had penetrated through to this very truth itself.

The awakening and teaching. And so Siddhartha sat and struggled with all kinds of inner conflicts and temptations, despair, and anxiety, until one morning, early, he saw the morning star rise; he saw it as though for the first and only time, with a clarity that surpassed any subjective apprehension. He saw it while, at the same time, being it, and being the vast space around it. He saw it without any separation. At that moment, in an instant, he went forward one further step and became deeply awakened. It was in that instant that he became Buddha.

His immediate reaction was to exclaim in joy, "Wonder of wonders, all beings, just as they are, are whole and complete. All beings can come to awakening." From this faith, a faith that goes beyond mere certainty and belief, he taught for many years, traveling all the while around India. He must have had an impressive demeanor because his very presence attracted crowds. His teaching was intensely practical, bearing a message of hope and compassion and concerned with showing the way beyond the suffering of life.

THE MEANING OF THIS STORY

The story of Buddha's life is of more than

historical value. Each of us has this potential for awakening and each of us, fearing the effort and pain that it seems to herald, tries to block out awareness of it. We live behind high walls of dogma and prejudice, trying to blind ourselves to the inexorable truth of life: that everything changes. The lot of all is sickness, old age, and death. Each of us has, in our own way, encounters with this truth: we fall sick, the decades slip by and we grow old, family and friends die. We know in our hearts that at its very foundation life is insecure and we retreat again and again to the illusory security of our daydream world. "Let us not think about this. Let us wait until it happens, then there will be time enough." But deep down the worm of doubt gnaws and the lives of most are filled with anxiety, unsteadiness, and restlessness.

There is an alternative to this. It is sometimes quite painful and difficult. But each of us has as our natural heritage the potential to awaken, and with this awakening is an end to suffering. Let us try to understand clearly what this means.

THE FOUR NOBLE TRUTHS

The fact of suffering. Suffering is a fact of life. This was the first lesson that Buddha taught. Suffering is neither an accident nor a punishment. To ask why we suffer is like asking why we breathe. There is a story that tells of a woman who went to Buddha, sometime after his great awakening, with her dead baby held in her arms. The baby had been bitten by a snake while playing. By going to Buddha she hoped to derive some solace and relief from her pain. Buddha said that he could help her, but first she should bring him a mustard seed from a house that had not known suffering. She went from house to house seeking such a seed but, although many offered seeds, she could not find a house that had not known suffering. So she returned to Buddha. He said:

My sister, thou hast found,
Searching for what none finds, that
    bitter balm
I had to give thee. He thou lovest slept
Dead on thy bosom yesterday; today
Thou knowest the whole world weeps
    with thy woe.

Release from suffering. It might seem pessimistic to talk this way. What good, it might be asked, is it to know that the foundation of life is suffering, that all without exception come to know suffering? Would it not be better to try to forget this and to look on the bright side? Yes, it would, if we could. But, alas, honesty and experience tell us that we cannot.

It is not only in Buddhism that one encounters

the need to open ourselves to the truth of suffering. There is an ancient hymn, attributed to Jesus, which says, "If you knew how to suffer, you would have the power not to suffer." If we deny suffering and claim that it is an accident or an intrusion, something that ought not to be, then we simply compound the problem. If suffering is there, real and true, no amount of denial will make it go away. But by opening ourselves to it, then there is at least a possibility we may come to know how to suffer and in this knowing transcend suffering. It was in the light of this transcendence that Buddha gave his first sermon. In this sermon he said that "All is suffering"; this was the first noble truth, an axiom of life. But it was not out of pessimism that Buddha spoke. He did not say, "There it is and there's nothing we can do about it but put up with it." He said, rather, that we must face the truth; it alone can set us free.

The third noble truth (leaving aside the second for a moment), says, equally clearly, that there is indeed a way out of suffering; we all potentially have the power not to suffer. However, to realize this potential we must take full responsibility for our suffering; this is the second noble truth. Suffering comes from craving, the craving to be an individual, even to be an immortal individual. Suffering does not have its origins outside of us. That its cause is not something done to us, that we are, in the end, responsible for it, this is the great teaching of Buddha. "By oneself," he said, "evil is done; by oneself one suffers; by oneself evil is undone; no one can purify another."

The craving to be separate and distinct colors all our life. It colors the way we see the world, what we try to do and what we say. It even affects the way we earn our living, while our ethics and conduct are also colored and distorted by it. This craving causes us to live asleep in a dream world in which our energies are dispersed and our attention scattered.

The way out of suffering was given by Buddha as the fourth noble truth, which has come to be known as the eightfold path, based upon the right way of seeing the world, or right view, right effort, speech, livelihood, conduct, and orientation. It is also based on right mindfulness and right concentration. It is these last two that Zen emphasizes, as we shall see later on. The word "right" does not mean right according to some perfect model or set of rules. Rather, it means without the distortion brought about by the craving to be separate. Right mindfulness and right concentration, for example, establish a steady and clear mind, which is the foundation for an ethical and spiritual life.

The truth of suffering resulting from our craving, and the possibility of transcending suffering by letting go of what distorts our relation to others and to the world, is the basis and motivation for spiritual effort. In one way or another this truth underlies Buddhist, Christian, and other spiritual endeavor. There are many ways to realize this truth and Zen is but one of these. However, Zen is a very vital and well-tried way and accessible to everyone to some degree. Let us therefore now turn specifically to Zen and try to understand more about it.

2

The Meaning of Zen

ZEN, CHAN, AND DHYANA

Zen is a Japanese word; indeed much of what we know about Zen has come to us from Japan, through the writings of a Japanese Zen Buddhist named D.T. Suzuki and through a number of dedicated Japanese and American Zen masters. However, Zen did not originate in Japan, but was imported from China, where it is known as Chan; Chan, in turn, was based on Buddhist practices that originated in India. The word Zen, or Chan, comes from the Sanskrit word *dhyana* meaning, loosely translated, meditation, as well as referring to a condition beyond subject and object. Tibet, Vietnam, Thailand, Cambodia, and Korea all have their own version of dhyana; it is a practice that has engaged many of the greatest minds of these ancient civilizations.

For many centuries we in the West have

tended to look down upon the East because we felt that our superiority in controlling and using the material forces of the world meant that we were in some way superior as human beings. More recently it has become apparent to many that, although Western civilization has indeed made miraculous progress in developing the physical sciences, nevertheless this has been done at the cost of neglecting another part of life, a part more human and intimate. It is precisely in this human, intimate, and, indeed, spiritual area that Zen has so much to offer.

BEYOND THE OPPOSITES

We have said that Zen came from the word dhyana, which could be said to mean beyond subject and object, that is, beyond distinguishing between "I" and "the world" or "I" and "it." Let us talk about this a little more.

Going beyond as going home. Most of us believe that the word "I" refers to something in us and that this something has a reality quite different from anything else. We believe also that the world, which we can call "it," has another kind of reality, which is quite different from the reality of "I," so different that the one is a stranger to the other. We take this for granted. We feel quite confident that "I" either is, or has,

something which we could, if we wanted to, uncover and know; and we also take it for granted
that a chair, a book, or a house is also a substance
that, provided we scratched below the surface, so
to speak, we could uncover and know. "I," we say,
is mind or soul or spirit, a finer substance; the
chair is matter, coarse and capable of being carved
up and used. If pressed, we would say, "I am
here" and "the world is out there" at the other
side of an abyss of separation. Even the body is
"out there," although admittedly there is a kind
of ambivalence surrounding this as we oscillate
between being the body and being in the body.

To talk of going beyond subject and object,
beyond "I" and "it," sounds somewhat abstract
and philosophical, and of little or no consequence
in our ordinary life. Endeavoring to go beyond
subject and object, one is inclined to feel, is all
right for mystics and others who are out of the
mainstream of real events. But for a manager, a
typist, a bricklayer, a salesperson, truck driver,
doctor, or lawyer, it would seem to be of little
value; staying afloat in the economic stream is a
full-time occupation and one that will suffer few
distractions.

However, a few moments' reflection will show
us that words, including words like "I" and "it,"
are themselves abstractions. They are convenient
tools and very useful in helping us to describe and
sort out what is happening around us, but they

are a convenience only. A car too is very useful, but to say that the only reality is that seen through its windshield would be an unnecessary limitation. This does not mean that we should ignore or deny this reality. Likewise, the view that is seen through the windshield of "I" and "it" is very useful, but to make this view the only possible one not only means that we are limiting ourselves unnecessarily, it also condemns us to some very painful enigmas—the most painful of all being the enigma of birth and death. If "I" is a reality separate from other realities, then we are inclined to ask: "Where was 'I' before birth and where will 'I' be after death?" As long as "I" is an independent something, separate from and even opposed to the "world," these questions must plague us: "Where did I come from? Where will I go? What is the meaning of this coming and going?" The problem of death is a very real one in our day and age and the meaning of death has become a central issue, so much so that the suppression and avoidance of the thought of death is a principal cause of neurosis and ungovernable anxiety.

If we consider "I" and the "world" to be real, any possibility of going beyond to an underlying unity is unreal. If, however, the underlying unity is real, then "I" and the "world" are just ways in which this unity shows itself, and the reality of "I" and the "world" is relative. To help make this point a little clearer, let us consider a cup. A cup has an inside and an outside, and these are quite different from each other. If one pours tea, for example, it obviously goes inside and not outside the cup. Inside and outside are two and distinct, but the cup is one. In a similar way, "I" and the "world" are two and quite different, yet there is one life. "I" could be looked upon as the "inside" of this life and the "world" as the "outside." We dwell always and only in the one life, but we are so absorbed in the illusion of "I" and so fascinated by the "world" that this unity is overlooked.

To say that "I" and the "world" are illusions is not to say that they do not exist, but rather that they do not exist in the way that we habitually believe they do, that is, as separate and discrete things. It is like going to the movies. We are totally fascinated by the moving pictures. We see the hero and heroine, we delight in their triumphs, and we feel sad at their failures. We are taken in by the show; we want to be taken in and we want the show to go on. When movie comes to an end, the film runs out and all that is left is the white light on the screen, which we ignore. And yet, after all, what so enthralled us was nothing other than variations of this light, shadows cast by it now being obscured and now clear. Moreover, as anyone knows who has seen a film made, these shadows are simply a patchwork of bits and pieces that we ourselves assemble into a whole. The white light is similar to the one life. The world that we know and feel and all that we ourselves are, are but modifications of this one life, shadows obscuring the light of this life. The shadows are there, they have their own existence, but they owe their reality to the white light.

Going beyond as home. Zen, or dhyana, is going beyond the opposites of "I and the world," of "life and death," of "here and there"—beyond all that can be described or even experienced. Of course, just as when we go beyond the inside and outside of the cup we do not really go anywhere but simply change perspective, so when we go beyond "I" and the "world" we do not go anywhere. This is important because some people feel that to meditate is to go out of yourself, or to go into a trance, or into higher levels of consciousness. But this is not so with Zen meditation. "I" and the "world" are ways of knowing. We can change the ways of knowing, but knowing itself remains unchanged. It is like clay: we can change its shape but the clay is always the same— it is always clay.

There is no reason to fear this going beyond, any more than there is reason to believe that it is either an exalted or an advanced state. It is neither the one nor the other. Most people have had some taste of it at least once or twice in their lives: a moment when falling in love, or hearing music and becoming the music, or being in the countryside and feeling the boundaries of space suddenly drop away, or a moment of extreme danger when everything seems to be timeless and yet everything is happening at once. It is a moment of deep calmness and peace—a moment of going beyond. It is quite natural, in the same way that going home is quite natural.

3

The Importance of Practice

ALL BEINGS ARE BUDDHA,
SO WHY NEED WE MEDITATE?

Dhyana, this unity beyond subject and object, is indeed always present, and is expressed in Buddhism by saying that we are already awakened. Not only all human beings, but all life is fully Buddha and therefore fully awakened, whole and complete just as it is. This is a very hard concept to understand; it seems to be one of those sayings that, because it says so much, says nothing. One is prompted to ask, "If we are already awakened, why must we meditate?" In truth, no one can answer this question satisfactorily; the only worthwhile answer is found in meditation itself.

Dogen, one of the greatest Japanese Zen masters, had a similar question. When he was three years old his mother died and when he was eight his father also died. Dogen felt very keenly the loss of his parents. When he grew up he became a Buddhist monk and heard it said that all beings are already awakened, fully enlightened. Remembering his pain, he asked, "Why then must I suffer? Why have all the Buddhas and patriarchs suffered so in the past?" It was this very question that drove him deeper into himself until he arrived at an answer. None of the teachers and masters that he met could give him an adequate reply.

Why do we need to meditate to come to awakening if we are already awakened? There is a simple experiment that can help point you in the right direction so that you can see for yourself why it is necessary: observe the second hand of a watch for two minutes, all the while remaining aware that you are observing. Only after you have tried this should you read on.

The stream of consciousness. What did you notice? Few people are able to observe the second hand for the full two minutes. Most, after a few seconds, find their thoughts carry them away and instead of observing the second hand, they end up wondering, "What is the point of this?" "What shall I do tonight?" "Shall I go on reading this?" "What is the use of reading anyway?" and so on. In short, they become lost in a stream of thoughts. But it is also important to notice that at some point before these thoughts begin to flow the mind is clear. And it is this moment of clarity that convinces many that the experiment is a waste of time—after all, nothing useful seems to be going on—and so they discontinue it.

This moment of clarity is a actually a hint that, in some way, we are already awakened. However, this clarity has also tricked us; it has caused us to discontinue the experiment. We reason that if we can suspend thought for a moment, we can suspend it for minutes, even hours if we really want to. But attempting to continue the experiment shows that this interlude of clarity is elusive and difficult to recover, that we are invariably carried away down the stream of thought. It is this that should convince us that some kind of inner work is necessary. These thoughts over which we have so little control, which are constantly swarming like bees, derive from a lifetime of emotion and tension. We are enslaved by them, and often so completely that we cannot even dream of a life free from them.

Still, the moment of clarity is very important; it shows, however vaguely, dimly, and imperfectly, that the stream of thought is not all. (It is also important to realize, however, that our little exercise is only an experiment and not a form of practice.) Clarity of awareness is not a thought, nor is it dependent upon a thought. On the contrary, thoughts are dependent upon, indeed are a form of, awareness. People often think they are the thoughts, that if the thoughts were to stop they would in some way disappear. But this is not so. We are that of which thoughts are made; we are awareness, unreflected awareness, "knowing" without form, limitless and timeless. It is from thoughts that the appearance of limitation arises. In this way they carry us away from clarity, just as clouds cover the sun although the sun continues to shine. All day long thoughts are streaming through the mind, and all day long we react to them—worry, anger, irritation, fear, hatred—a continuous reaction to this stream of thought.

Clarity is thus not only obscured by the images and forms, thoughts and judgments that flow through the mind, but also by our emotional reaction to them. Furthermore, we are constantly trying to make sense of all these thoughts and emotions, trying to sort them out and put them in order. It is like trying to sort out a mixture of jigsaw puzzles that have many parts missing and whose available parts are constantly changing shape and relation to each other. So we try to impose our will upon the pieces and force them into definite shapes. We try to combine them or separate them by an effort of will, try deliberately to make some things happen and to stop others from happening. It is this effort of will that splits things up into "this and that," "me and you," and so on. It is, furthermore, this total confusion of jigsaw puzzles that we call consciousness, which also, although arising originally out of clear knowing, now obscures this clarity.

The five *skandhas*.   Our inner life has been called by Buddhists a bitter ocean of life and death. Life and death here means beginning and ending or, better still, arising and passing away. Someone characterized life as "one damned thing after another" because there is so often a bitter quality, even a painful quality about these arisings and passings away. So often we seem to be in over our heads and struggling to get on our feet. No sooner have we accomplished this than we find ourselves swept along by another wave. The ocean is restless, sometimes with high waves following one after the other, sometimes calm. But even when calm it is never still. This churning comes from our emotions, from our striving and effort and from our grasping and rejecting, picking and choosing, indeed from the very nature of consciousness itself, which, even when clear of thought and feeling, nevertheless ebbs and flows constantly like waves on the beach. These five— form, feeling, thought, will, and consciousness— are called in Buddhism the five *skandhas*, or five sheaths, that obscure our true nature. During meditation the nonreality of these five sheaths is seen into. Later it is seen that, although they obscure clear knowing, they are even so themselves ways through which clear knowing shows itself. Then this clear knowing itself is seen into. It is something like the shapes of jugs, plates, cups, and teapots—they are all ways that clay can show itself. While we are intent upon the forms and the uses that these forms can be put to, we do not see the clay; but if we see the clay, we are no longer taken in by the forms. Then, later still, we see into the nature of clay itself.

Emptiness. We could again use the metaphor of a movie to show from a different angle what is meant by seeing into the nonreality of things. The individual frames that make up a movie are projected onto a screen and they have a certain opaqueness or solidity. If, however, a light were to be thrown onto the back of the screen, this opaqueness and solidity would diminish. The film would go on unchanged, but we should not be taken in so completely by it. Clear awareness faithfully reflects all that appears and this appearance at its own level has a solidity and opaqueness that we call reality. However, awareness can be aroused and experience then loses its opaque and solid quality.

This loss of opaqueness in experience enables us to see in another way that things are not quite what they seem: they are not separate and isolated, but interdependent with everything else. A chair, for example, is dependent upon the sun or lamp for its color, upon gravity for its weight, upon air for its smell, upon all other things for its location in space and time, and so on. Indeed, by way of this analysis we find our conviction that the chair is something existing in and for itself is called into question. Even more is this conviction undermined when we remember that the chair cannot be seen, felt, or experienced in any way unless there is someone there to experience it.

THE DIFFICULTY OF MEDITATION

Seeing into the emptiness, the shadowlike quality of conscious experience, is not easy. Although we can arrest the flow of thoughts momentarily whenever we like, we must not delude ourselves that this betokens any kind of control. Indeed, the first lesson that we learn when we practice meditation is that we do not have any control at all over thoughts and that we are entirely at their mercy. This is true whether we see ourselves as just ordinary people or as particularly important, clever, creative, or strong-willed. Indeed, it might be true that those who see themselves as ordinary people have the easiest time of it.

Some people who come to meditation feel that the cause of all these thoughts and the cause of their having so little control lies in the meditation itself, and so are put off. However, meditation is like turning on a light in a roomful of junk; it is only when the light is on, however feebly it may shine, that we can see how confused and untidy the room is. Naturally, at times, meditation will be hard. This too causes some people to be dismayed, because they have been led to believe that meditation should be easy, relaxing, and fulfilling. However, while at a deep level there is undoubtedly a sense of fulfillment and rightness in meditation, nevertheless at the surface, where most of us, to begin with, apply all our attention, it sometimes seems dry, frustrating, and demanding. However, one should not be discouraged by this; one should not feel during these dry, difficult times that one has taken the wrong path or is doing the wrong thing; nor should one look for another, "more interesting," way.

This misunderstanding about meditation has come about partly because of some early misconceptions about Zen, partly because of some misunderstandings about meditation in general, and partly out of the tendency inherent in us all to look for the easy way out. In order to clarify this, we will need to understand some basic terms a little more fully, the concern of the next chapter.

4

Ingredients of Practice

Zen, we said earlier, comes from the Sanskrit word *dhyana*, which can be translated as "beyond subject and object." Previously we said that it could be loosely translated "meditation" but, as we shall see, this can lead us into difficulties. So instead of meditation we shall use the Japanese word *zazen*, for which there is no exact English equivalent (in Japanese, *za* means sitting). Actually, zazen has three aspects, only one of which is meditation; the other two are concentration and contemplation.

Concentration. Concentration means "with a center" ("con," meaning with, plus center); thus, to concentrate means to bring all the contents of conscious experience into harmony with a common center. This requires very intense effort, which most people can sustain for only brief periods of time. This center may be anything: a sound that is repeated, a mantra, a single thought, or even pain. Concentration has great value because it summons up a natural energy. This could be called the energy of oneness. In Japanese it is called *joriki*.

The word "healing" comes from the same root as the word "whole." When we are scattered, our minds fragmented and dispersed, we fall away from wholeness and health. To bring the mind to one-pointedness is a natural way to heal the mind and to maintain mental health. But this healing requires energy, or joriki, which is generated by concentration. Furthermore, unless we are able to concentrate the mind to some extent, we are unable to do anything of our own volition, and are thus dependent upon the environment to stimulate us in new ways so that we can maintain interest. This applies to zazen as well. We learn to concentrate the mind by doing zazen, but to do this we must put out a certain amount of energy and put up with a certain amount of discomfort, even pain. However, concentrating is not unlike paying off a mortgage on a house—for some time we simply pay off the interest and scarcely any of the principal is touched. A debt has been accumulated through failure to live according to the eightfold path. As time goes by we are able to pay off more and more of the debt itself until eventually we become free. Paying off the interest is overcoming the restlessness and distraction; paying off the debt is the steady transformation of our lives starting at the deepest levels.

The idea that pain can be used as a center for concentration is very important, and as it may be a new and possibly disturbing thought to some people, let us talk a little more about it. Pain has often been used and inflicted over the history of mankind to bring about a concentrated state of mind. Initiation ceremonies, vows, and prayers are often accompanied by pain, partly because this helps to bring the mind to one-pointedness. This one-pointedness in turn releases a great deal of mental energy. This mental energy can then be used to "fix," so to speak, that upon which attention is focused. In Tibetan and Zen Buddhism, pain is looked upon as an ally, and in Tibetan Buddhism methods are sometimes used to induce pain. For the Westerner, the postures that are adopted for zazen are often painful and the practitioner will often be encouraged to "use the pain to help in the practice." The release of energy that comes from pain can be a great help in other aspects of the practice. And it is not only physical pain that can be used in this way, but emotional pain as well, such as the feeling of *angst* so familiar to many people.

Many Westerners, who do not see the value of a clear mind and who in any case could never contemplate a positive and constructive use of pain, would consider this use of pain a form of masochism. Masochism, however, is the enjoyment of pain for its own sake, while we are talking about the transmutation of pain, physical or mental, into vital energy. As one concentrates, pain becomes more and more refined and it is accepted in a more integrated and relaxed manner; less and less effort is therefore required and a heightened sense of togetherness can ensue. Some say that the energy developed in this way can also be used to develop powers of extra-sensory perception. This may be so, although ways that claim to develop such powers for their own sake should be viewed with considerable skepticism. In Buddhism the development of such powers is not encouraged because true spiritual development does not lie in this direction.

Meditation. The word meditation means to "think about" or "ponder on." It is a basic practice in most religions, including Buddhism. In the early stages, meditation can be accompanied by reading. This kind of reading, however, is not undertaken for the sake of getting information or knowledge, but as a stimulus to aid one to intuitively understand what is being read; therefore, the only worthwhile writings for meditation are those of spiritually developed people. All religions have sacred scripture, as well as books written by and about deeply enlightened or spiritually developed people. Meditation in this instance, therefore, means reading phrases or paragraphs of these works and allowing their import to sink in deeply. This has the effect of breaking up the hard crust of the mind and softening the heart, which allows the deep need we all have for some total fulfillment to rise more readily to the surface. Care, of course, must be taken when meditating not to allow oneself to be carried away. The softening of the heart is often accompanied by a deep easing, and a soothing feeling. If this is sought after for its own sake it can easily degenerate into a cloying sweetness. However, after very intense periods of concentration, during difficult times of dryness and pain, or through periods of loss and extreme bewilderment, meditation can be of great value.

Contemplation. Contemplation is the main practice of Zen. The Sanskrit word for this is *prajna*. *Jna* is primordial knowing, a knowing that is non-reflective; *pra* means aroused or awakened. Thus prajna is the state or activity of being aroused or awakened to that which simply "is." In English translation, however, the term is liable to be misunderstood, so before defining it, we might specify first what contemplation is not.

The expression "to contemplate one's navel" is often used to disparage the practice of zazen.

This phrase implies a dreamy, vacuous mind-state stemming from an inert passivity. Even non-perjorative uses of the word, such as in the expression "contemplating nature," still have this passive connotation. What we are referring to by contemplation is a passive state but also, and at the same time, an intensely active condition.

The Japanese word *shikan-taza* can be translated as "just sitting." Some teachers of Zen prescribe this practice for anyone, beginners or otherwise. However, shikan-taza is pure contemplation and is, for those who have not spent a number of years practicing, far too difficult. Most often people who think they are practicing shikan-taza are sitting in a state in which they are simply aware of their own reflected consciousness. Even though this consciousness may be reflected by nothing in particular, nevertheless such practice is by and large a useless kind of exercise and can have no real value.

Contemplation is without a center and is therefore not concentration, although it has all the intensity of concentration. It has no thought, and so is not meditation, although it has all the flexibility and ease of meditation. Clear attention, simple awareness without reflection, is knowing without a subject who knows, nor object that is known. As such it is "an aroused mind that rests on nothing" (the theme of one of the most celebrated scriptures of Zen, *The Diamond Sutra*).

What must be emphasized, however, is that this aroused mind is only present in glimpses or flashes, not as a constant state. A French writer on Zen Buddhism, Hubert Benoit, refers to it as an "inner glance." Although contemplation is lending oneself unremittingly to clear awareness, this latter for a long time is present only as is black lightning on a dark night. Described in words, such a state seems remote and difficult to attain—perhaps even inaccessible. The difficulty arises in the first place because what is being described is so intimate, so ever present, that it is constantly overlooked; in the second place, true contemplation is upstream of all thoughts, ideas, and words, and can be only alluded to at best. However, faithful and devoted practice of the kind suggested in this book will allow what is being referred to to reveal itself—shyly at first, and delicately, but with ever increasing luster and sureness.

Dhyana. Because we have been able to talk about concentration, meditation, and contemplation separately, we must not fall into the error of believing that they are separate "faculties." Rather, it is a question of emphasis upon one or another aspect of a fundamental attitude of faith. When the mind is very restless, then concentration above all is called for; when a particular insight or understanding occurs or is sought, then meditation above all is required; when moments of clarity and togetherness occur, then this is contemplation. However, one should not be asking oneself, "Should I now be meditating or contemplating?" The distinction should be understood, then forgotten. Together, concentration, meditation, and contemplation are dhyana, and it is dhyana that provides the foundation for the moment of awakening, in Japanese, *satori*, which can be very roughly translated "seeing into in a flash."

FAITH, DOUBT, AND PERSEVERANCE

Faith. To practice Zen, to undertake this work, which may be hard and long, requires great faith. This does not mean faith in miracles or dogma, or in something that others have seen or realized. Rather, it is faith that one can indeed work with, and so go beyond, the confusion and pain of life. For many people faith entails a kind of bargain: "I'll have faith if you promise to release me from the calamities of life." The proof of this is found in the fact that many, when calamity strikes, lose their faith, thinking, "What is the use of faith if this can happen to me?" Faith, however, does not promise escape from calamity, but rather faith is the means to bear any calamity, no matter how severe. *Knowing* is indestructible; *faith* is this indestructibility in action. Faith that one can go beyond the confusion is faith in this indestructible knowing—this knowing that each essentially "is"—is not born and does not die.

Faith is essential. Without it one cannot make a move. If one practices zazen without faith, it will be mechanical, in the manner of a merchant who wants something and has something to trade for it: "I'll do two hours of zazen if you will give me a good feeling all day," or "if you will take away my sickness," or "if you will make me omniscient," or "if you will fill me with peace and joy," or whatever. Such zazen inevitably leads into a cul-de-sac. It is dry and self-serving, and the practitioner will always be sitting outside his or her own gate, waiting to be allowed in. It is zazen prompted by some outside force or example. People who practice in this manner are very often initially "sold" on the idea of Zen. They then cling to a teacher or a Zen center, demanding that one or the other or both *do* something for them, and when, as they say, "nothing happens," they blame both the teacher and the teaching.

Faith and belief are frequently confused. We believe in ideas or scriptures or the words of others. When we believe, we invest our faith and give it a specific form, but at the same time we immobilize it. If faith could be looked upon as a flashing sword cutting through all confusion and doubts, belief could be considered that same sword in its scabbard.

In one way it can be said that all have faith.

Even the catatonic curled up in a corner has faith invested in the belief that this posture, this dark corner, will protect him from the pain that is so bad. To get out of bed, to meet others, to walk or run, all of this is the activity of faith. But, through beliefs, convictions, and prejudices we limit, channel, and dam our faith, and so we come to the point where we say we lack faith. When this seems to be the case we should unlock the gates of beliefs and break down the dams of prejudice, walk through the walls of convictions. Meditation on the sayings of a great teacher whom one finds inspiring is of great value in this. To read and dwell upon the sayings can help greatly. Just read a few lines and allow the meaning to soak in, allow the significance of the truth to seep through gently. Do not be in a hurry. Meditating is like watering dry earth—it takes time for the green shoots to appear.

Doubt. Faith, however, is not enough; along with great faith there must be great doubt. Paradoxically, it is only those who have great faith who can truly doubt. Without faith, doubt will simply degenerate into skepticism. Great doubt begins with doubting oneself, doubting the very foundation upon which this self is based. It means doubting one's most cherished beliefs, the most self-evident axioms. Without great faith, this can be both difficult and dangerous. A skeptic, on the other hand, simply doubts what others say; he or she is very defensive and has no true base from which to doubt. The skeptic has no true faith.

Great doubt is not simply an intellectual searching, although it may begin as such. It is rather a willingness to open oneself to doubts that already exist. We live our lives, as it were, trying to seal up the gaps in the walls of prejudice and opinion that we have built around ourselves. The world and others, most often inadvertently and without malice, expose the cracks, the uncertainties, and inconsistencies in these walls that we have built. Our thinking is invariably concerned with sealing up these cracks and with giving reasons for the inconsistencies, and hence with blocking out uncertainties. It is with this that most of the restless agitation of our mind is concerned. We are anxious about what others think of us, what they might or might not do; we are anxious about what will become of us. We are worried that two people might get together and betray to each other the secrets we have confided to each. We are worried about the pain in our chest or in our head. We are concerned about the future and troubled about the past, and the present is somewhat unsatisfactory. It is all of this that we try to exclude with the walls we build.

Great doubt is simply, to begin with, letting go of the struggle to seal up the cracks, allowing the walls to crumble and slide. It is declining to follow through with the reasons that offer themselves as salve to the pain we feel about what someone said or did that upset us. It is seeing, without blaming others or retreating into shame, that the bluster we present in the face of criticism is but a trick. With great doubt the truth that all of our suffering is self-inflicted is allowed to surface and at the same time the needlessness of our striving to avoid suffering and to blame others is acknowledged. Great doubt is painful, but the more we allow it just to be, the more great faith will shine through; and the more great faith shines through, the more daring we can become in widening the crack of the door to our innermost heart.

We need have no fear. Anything that arises in the process of doing zazen will be taken away by zazen. In the words of T.S. Eliot, to be cured, "our sickness must grow worse," and yet, while being the patient, we are forever the physician.

Great perseverance. But, of course, as we have said, we must persevere. If we wish to perfect ourselves as a violinist, a runner, an artist, a singer, or a practitioner of any other discipline, we must give up time and devote energy. We must go through difficult times and pleasant times, times of hope and times of despair. And so it is with the practice of zazen, which is the perfection of that which is most truly perfect. It is best not to count the cost, not to remember how much one has done or how much one has still to do. Be concerned only with what is here and now to be done. We should not, moreover, attempt to judge how well we are doing, for with each improvement our expectations will increase accordingly. Great perseverance is staying with the practice moment by moment, day by day, year by year; our perseverance can in fact only be called great when, rather than trying to fit the practice somewhere into our life, we see the whole of life as one practice.

PART II
Practice

5

Beginning to Practice

It is now time to consider more carefully how Zen is practiced. It has been necessary for us to spend time showing what zazen means because without such orientation we cannot truly understand what we must do. Without understanding the "why," it is difficult to follow the "how." However, once we have started on the "how", the "why" becomes of less importance. It is not necessary for one to keep up the scaffolding once the house has been built. In Zen it is said that one must not confuse the moon with the finger that points to the moon; no amount of theory will ever take the place of even a few minutes of practice.

POSTURE

Importance of posture. In the West, the way one sits to study or kneels to pray is unimportant. What is important is the application of one's mind or heart. This, however, reveals our very profound sense of duality and our belief that the body is, at best, an encumbrance, at worst, a hindrance to the flight of mind or soul. In the practice of Zen, however, it is precisely the illusion of this duality that is seen as the primary hindrance, and consequently the positioning of the body is as important as the fixing of the mind or the steadying of the heart. The body is not opposed to the mind, although the two are obviously different. A rough analogy might be a hammer and the blow of a hammer. These are obviously different, and yet by no means separate or opposed.

Sitting in a prescribed fashion with a correct posture is always stressed in Zen Buddhism. It is remarkable that the way my teacher, Roshi Philip Kapleau, taught me to sit in zazen is identical to the way Dogen, a Japanese Zen master who lived about eight hundred years ago, taught his students, and the tradition was already ancient when Dogen was teaching. This is stressed, because it is important for us to realize that the teaching of authentic Zen Buddhism is not some new idea that someone is experimenting with, but has roots in an ancient teaching whose value has been attested to by the experience of countless millions of people.

Straight back and low center of gravity. Basic to the meditation posture is a straight back and a

Fig. 1. A correct posture for zazen.

low center of gravity (Fig. 1). By a straight back is meant one that is supported by the spinal column alone. From the drawing of the spinal column (Fig. 2), it can be seen that there is a natural curve at A. A straight back is one in which the whole weight of the torso is supported by this curve. If

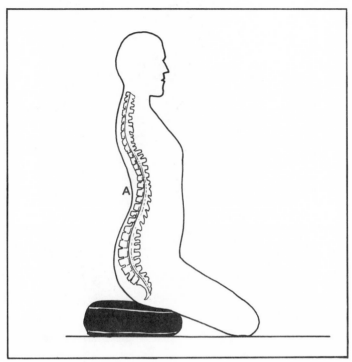

Fig. 2. The natural curve of the spinal column.

the shoulders or head are tilted forward, then it will not be possible for this curve to do its work (Fig. 3). Therefore, after sitting down to practice zazen, it is important that the buttocks should be raised off the cushion and pushed back (Fig. 4). This will have the effect of tilting the pelvis forward when one sits. The reason one sits on a cushion is precisely to make use of this curve. If one sits on the floor directly, without a cushion,

Fig. 3. Incorrect posture.

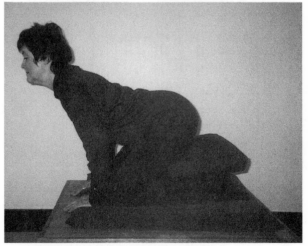

Fig. 4. Getting into the correct position.

then it is virtually impossible to achieve a straight back—even if one is able to adopt the full lotus posture. To give adequate support, the cushion should be firm, preferably stuffed with kapok, not with feathers or foam.

When seated properly, one's center of gravity should be that point at which all of the forces at work in the body naturally meet. This point, called *tanden* in Japanese, is about an inch or more below the navel. However, more generally it is said that this center of gravity is located in the *hara*, the abdominal region. This is is a very important area, but we shall defer saying more about it until later, when we can deal with the topic fully. For the moment, let us say only that a straight back will allow a low center of gravity to develop naturally and this low center will, in its turn, be of considerable aid in carrying on the practice while maintaining a good posture.

The word *naturally* should be emphasized. At first, sitting on the floor on a cushion with the legs crossed may seem to be very unnatural. However, this is because of the training and conditioning that we undergo in the West. After one has mastered the posture, it becomes apparent that sitting in a chair, particularly in a slumped posture, is what is unnatural.

The lotus posture. To attain the lotus posture, the legs should be crossed, with the left foot on

Fig. 5. The full-lotus posture.

the right thigh and the right foot on the left thigh
(Fig. 5). If this is done correctly, the knees rest on
the floor quite firmly. The two knees and the buttocks make a tripod that naturally supports the
body. This is called the full-lotus posture.
However, most Westerners find this too difficult
and *on no account should one force oneself to
adopt this posture.* To do so might cause all kinds
of unnecessary problems.

Fig. 6. The half-lotus posture.

Even if one cannot attain the full-lotus posture, one may be able to adopt the half-lotus posture. This is a posture in which the left foot is put on the right thigh, and the right heel is tucked under the left leg, touching or almost touching the crotch (Fig. 6). Or, one can use the Burmese

Fig. 7. The Burmese posture.

posture (Fig. 7), in which the left foot is not put on the right thigh but alongside the right leg.

The hands and the head. The hands are placed in a special position. The right hand should rest open, palm up, with the fingers pointing to the left. The back of the left hand should rest upon

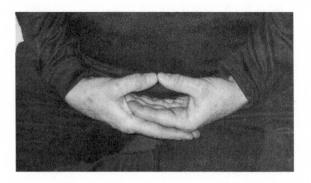

Fig. 8. Correct hand position.

the right, fingers pointing to the right. The thumbs should be touching each other very lightly—barely touching and yet not quite separate. This injunction about the thumbs is important. In zazen the hands should be vital, alive (Fig. 8). This initially is clearly expressed in the way the hands are held. If the thumbs are pressed together to make a steeple, the posture is too tight and tense (Fig. 9). If the thumbs are lifeless and fall apart, the posture is too slack (Fig. 10).

The position of the head is also important. If it is allowed to hang forward and down, one has adopted a posture of defeat (see Fig. 3); if it is allowed to fall back on the neck, it is a posture of weakness (Fig. 11). It is a good idea to get

Fig. 9. Hands held too closely.

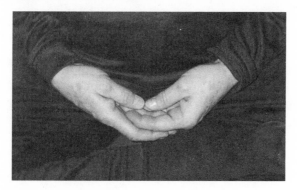

Fig. 10. Hands held too loosely.

someone, preferably someone who is knowledgeable about the matter, to position the head correctly for you the first time so that you will know how it feels. To assure that the head is correctly positioned, one should look straight

Fig. 11. Incorrect head position.

ahead and sight a spot to confirm that the position is right. After the head is in the correct position, the eyelids should be dropped with the eyes open, but unfocused. It is important to keep the eyes open because by closing them we are indicating that what is important is "inside" and that we can therefore ignore the "outside." This brings up and reinforces the latent dualism. Keeping the eyes unfocused prevents them from becoming strained, and also helps avoid the unpleasant visual effects that can be produced if one stares.

The kneeling posture. Some people find the half lotus too difficult and so are advised to try one of the kneeling positions. The kneeling posture is used by those practicing the martial arts—aikido, karate, swordsmanship and so on—although those practitioners do not use cushions as is done in Zen. Essentially, the posture is attained as follows: kneel down, sitting on the heels. The knees should be about two fists apart and the feet about one. *Between* the feet and the buttocks, put a hard cushion (Fig. 12). Preferably this should be a husk cushion, husks being firmer even than kapok; it should not be a feather or foam cushion. If you are not able to obtain a husk cushion, use a tightly rolled-up blanket. Across the cushion or blanket place another small flat kapok cushion on which to sit. The combined height of the two cushions should be such that you are sitting slightly higher than your feet. In this way the blood can circulate freely. The positioning of the hands and head and the movement to ensure the spine is correct is the same as for the lotus posture. Note the position of the feet. By allowing the feet to slightly overlap the edge of

Fig. 12. Using a hard cushion.

the mat the natural contours of the feet are followed and so the posture is more comfortable.

Sitting on a chair. If you have difficulty with
the kneeling posture also, you can find or make a
small bench. This can be used to sit on in a kneeling position, without any weight being placed on

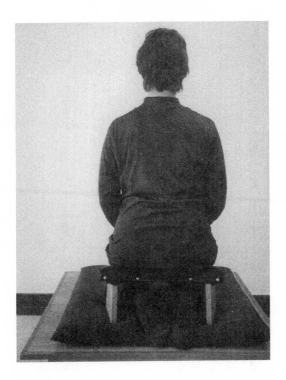

Fig. 13. Using a bench.

the legs or feet (Fig. 13). If this too is uncomfortable, then you should practice sitting on a chair (Fig. 14). If you do sit on a chair the following points are important. The chair should be of a height that will allow the thighs to be horizontal and the feet to be placed firmly on the floor. It should not slope back and it should be firm;

Fig. 14. Using a chair.

folding chairs are not good. One should sit upright, not rest the back against the chair. If one has back trouble, a cushion can be wedged between the small of the back and the back of the chair. The knees should be apart and the feet placed at an angle of "ten minutes to two." The hands should be placed in the lap.

Sitting on a mat. In a Zen center one usually sits on a mat made with cotton batting covered with cotton material, about thirty-two inches square. This protects the legs and knees. Sitting upon a hard floor is not recommended. In the absence of a sitting mat, a soft carpet, folded blanket, or sleeping bag will do.

Settling into the posture. Take time when sitting down to ensure that you are comfortable. A period of sitting usually lasts from twenty to forty minutes and you should be as comfortable as possible. After you have taken up your posture, rock from side to side and to and fro slightly so that you may be sure that you are sitting upright. After you have practiced for a while you will have no difficulty in determining an upright posture. Take a deep breath or, if you like, sigh deeply, at the beginning of the practice period. To straighten the upper part of the spinal column, the chin should be in. To achieve this, rather than deliberately pulling the chin into the chest, which will cause strain, imagine for a moment that you are going to touch the ceiling with the top of your head.

Before leaving the question of posture. It should be stressed that, although the posture is very important, it is simply an aid. In other words, one should not get hung up about the posture, wishing that one could get into some posture that is at present too difficult to attain. The most important thing is to maintain a straight back and low center of gravity.

PRACTICE

Breath practice. Once you have found the best posture for yourself and have adopted it, you are ready to begin zazen practice. The basic method is very simply stated: one counts the breath, one for the first in-breath, two for the out-breath, three for the next in-breath, four for the out-breath, and so on, up to ten. At ten, start again with one and continue as before. When you are quite comfortable with counting in- and out-breaths, then count out-breaths only.

Because this method is so simply stated, many may be seduced into believing that it is easily done. However, this is not so and it might be as well to give a little background to the practice to understand why it is not.

Mindfulness. The basis of Buddhist practice is mindfulness. It is desirable to be mindful at all times. By mindful is meant acting, talking, and thinking from a clear mind; it means to have clear awareness, which entails letting go of the struggle to seal up the cracks. We have discussed this earlier, but let us review the point here again because it is important to understand what is intended in practice.

Most people, if one were to ask them "Who (or what) are you really?" would answer that they are the "body" or the "mind," or perhaps "soul," or even "spirit." When pressed, it soon becomes evident that the question completely stymies them. On the one hand, it is so obvious to them who or what they are; on the other hand, what they say they are is something they have simply accepted, perhaps through reading or due to a generally held belief. They cannot really define what they are clearly.

We can demonstrate this for ourselves simply by trying to answer the question. For each of us, the answer to "What am I?" is a mystery, a truth that we know but cannot put into any kind of expression or form. Still, we are constantly striving to find a such form. The search for meaning of Victor Frankl, for identity of Erik Eriksen, for individuation of Jung, for the will to power of Nietzsche, not to mention the search for the Holy Grail, Shambala, the Promised Land, Heaven, etc.—all can be shown to have as their basis this urge to give form to that which has no form.[1] Mindfulness, or clear attention, is to be no longer addicted to finding the form.

---

[1] For more on this subject, see *The Iron Cow of Zen*, by Albert Low (Wheaton, Ill.: Quest Publishing, 1985).

Following and counting the breath. Practice is, therefore, mindfulness. The most profound practice of all is shikan-taza, just sitting, just knowing. However, as we learned through the experiment with the watch, it is difficult to do this for even a minute or so without being carried away by all kinds of thoughts and ideas. So to help us, Zen masters advise us to "follow the breath," or to "contemplate the breath." Each in-breath is the first and only, each out-breath is the first and only; there is no gap between the in-breath and the out-breath—they are one breath. To do this it is necessary to follow the breath all the way out, until it is not obvious whether one is breathing out or in, then to follow the breath all the way in. One must not get caught up in the physiology of breathing; do not imagine, for example, the current of breath entering the nostrils and going down into the lungs and so on. It is much better to breathe through the knees and elbows, through the soles of the feet and the palms of the hands. In other words, be totally involved. But remember that this following the breath is an aid—there is no magic or mystique.

If you have not practiced Zen before it is preferable for you to count the breath during the first three months or so of your practice. To do this you count "one" as you breathe out, "two" as you breathe in, "three" out and so on up to ten. Then start again with "one." The counting should be concurrent with the breathing; in other words, all the time you are breathing out you should be counting "one"; all the time you are breathing in count "two" and so on. If you give your full attention to this practice you will find that the thoughts will drop away without your doing anything about them.

It is important not to deliberately block thoughts as they arise. This will not assist your efforts at all. After a short while your mind will wander. Do not be too hard on yourself. Rather, quietly return to one and start again. Success is not getting to ten; success is patiently, persistently returning, again and again, to the practice. Also, do not get caught up in visualizing numbers. *The answer to a wandering mind is to arouse the mind.* A word of caution should be added: beware of sitting with the *idea* of following the breath. Although it is difficult to do otherwise to begin with, nevertheless one should be aware that our practice is calling us to break through this barrier of ideas.

Posture and breath practice.   Correct posture also is an aid to following and counting the breath. When the back is straight and the center of gravity low, the body is virtually supported by the spinal column alone. The muscles of the upper body can therefore be quite relaxed—particularly the muscles of the neck and shoulders.

This, in turn, means that the attention is free and not directed toward knotted tensions here and there throughout the body.

Furthermore, correct posture allows the diaphragm to be quite free. This is important because with this freedom one is able to use the stomach muscles to help with the breathing and so it becomes deeper and slower. It is said that the average person breathes from twelve to fourteen times per minute. For an experienced Zen practitioner this would be panting. Eight to ten times is quite sufficient, once one is able to breathe using the diaphragm and abdominal muscles. Indeed, during the very deep zazen that is possible during retreats, one may sometimes breath about once a minute or even less.

The benefits of this deeper breathing are manifold. Chest breathing is mainly emergency breathing. One only has to think of the heaving breast of anger, grief, or excitement to realize this. To breathe all the time using emergency breathing means one is always on edge, in an unnatural state of tension. Simply by using the stomach to breath, one can experience a release of tension, a calmness and poise not known before. Furthermore, a greater portion of the capacity of the lungs is used, so the system can adjust more readily to the needs for more or less oxygen. The body's metabolism can in this way be more finely tuned to the needs of the situation, and so the body becomes healthier at a very fundamental level. There have been a number of studies carried out on the physiological benefits of this slower, deeper breathing.[2]

A word of caution. The practice described above is to *follow* the breath, not to control it or to lead it. The very delicate balance between oxygen and carbon dioxide must be maintained if the organism is to function efficiently. There is a profound wisdom of the body. It is the same wisdom that presided over its evolution and regulates its birth, growth, and development; it is the wisdom that makes the body well during sickness and that heals the body when it is wounded—the same wisdom that is called upon by genuine faith healers. It is this wisdom also that maintains the balance of breath. It is best not to change the rhythm of the breath intentionally, for example, to try to breathe more deeply or more slowly. The body has its reasons for breathing slowly or less slowly, deeply or less deeply. Zazen practice is to tune into the rhythm, to be sensitive to it, to let it happen.

Of course, the very act of paying attention to the breath changes the breath. However, this is

[2]See, for example, *Science and the Evolution of Consciousness*, by Dr. Hiroshi Motoyama with Rande Brown (Autumn Press, 1978), and *Zen Meditation Therapy* by Tomio Hirai (Tokyo: Japan Publications, 1975).

not too important as it is only temporary; when one becomes used to the practice this will not happen. What is undesirable as a practice is to deliberately breathe deeply or slowly, or to hold the breath or try to use the abdomen to breathe and so on. After all, as mentioned previously, the practice is to cultivate clear attention to whatever is; this clear attention can hardly be maintained if we are full of ideas and thoughts about breathing.

The practice of counting or following the breath should be done in the zazen posture; it is not desirable to do it while walking around. We will talk more about this later, but here it is as well to point out that the need for the body to make subtle shifts and changes in breathing is more likely to arise when in action than when sitting still. Consequently, the likelihood increases, as one becomes more active, of the practice of following or counting the breath interfering with one's breathing.

Hara. With an upright posture and proper breathing, *hara* may be developed. Hara is a Japanese word that means "belly." This region is considered the source of initiative or action, a concept that is unknown or underemphasized in the West. However, it is of some interest to note that this region in the pelvic basin is called the sacral region, named after the sacrum, that part of the spinal column adjoined to the pelvis. Sacrum has the same root as "sacred," suggesting that at one time this area had some special significance. In the West, some teachers of ballet and singing encourage their students to have the source of their movements in this hara region. In the East much more emphasis is placed upon it—especially in the martial arts.

The hara is the whole pelvic region, but there is one particular point called the *tanden,* situated a couple of inches below the navel, that calls for special comment. The tanden is the point on which all the forces of the body tend naturally to focus if allowed to function in an entirely natural way. This natural functioning is not simply physical, but psychological also, and indeed can only arise when the tendency to see mind and body as two distinct, separate fields is dropped. To act naturally is to act without this artificial distinction between body and mind—without the belief that, for example, the mind must control or discipline the body, or that the body is some kind of prison or container for the mind. When acting naturally, the psycho-physical force (that the Japanese call *ki,* as in Aikido), centers in the hara without effort. This in turn brings about an effortless concentration that arises because all local conflicts and tensions are released in favor of the tautness and power of ki.

Again, the emphasis is upon *natural.* Hara cannot be developed by pushing attention down into the hara. This is quite contrary to the whole spirit of hara, which, as stated previously, is that the source of initiative lies in hara. To push down into the hara means in effect that the source of initiative is in the head or chest. Furthermore, although the development of hara and the associated development of psycho-physical force (or concentration energy) is a great help, both in the practice of Zen and in everyday life, it is important that it should not become an end in itself, as this too can become its own kind of distraction. The development of hara alone is not sufficient to bring us to awakening.

The half smile. Another aspect of zazen that should be emphasized is the half smile. If you observe a good Buddha or bodhisattva image closely, you will notice that the mouth tends toward a smile; "tends toward" is used because one cannot really say the figure is smiling. This facial expression is related to an incident in the life and teaching of Buddha that has a special significance in Zen. According to tradition, Buddha was called upon to give a talk to a large assembly of monks and lay people. Everyone present was anxious to hear what he had to say because he was known as one who could be both eloquent and incisive. However, on this occasion, instead of giving a long talk, Buddha simply held up a flower. All the monks, except one, were taken aback by this gesture and were unsure what to do or think. Mahakasyapa, a senior disciple of Buddha, alone smiled. At this, Buddha proclaimed that he had transmitted the teaching to Mahakasyapa.

This story has a special interest for Zen, for it is said that with this incident the Zen tradition had its beginning. The story is in full accord with the fundamental understanding of Zen that truth cannot be realized by thoughts, images, or words. It is much more immediate than this. Birds can be said to live in the air, fish in water, but mankind lives in truth. It could be said that Mahakasyapa saw the truth directly when Buddha held up the flower. But what is important at this time is the fact that on seeing the truth, Mahakasyapa smiled. He was not smiling at Buddha nor smiling to himself. When we are entirely one with a situation we tend to smile. For example, when we are with friends or when we listen to music that absorbs us, or when we hear good news, or see into some new truth, we are more likely to be at one with the situation and less likely to want to avoid it or separate ourselves from it. This feeling goes along with the tendency to smile. If we sit and allow the lips to curve a little at the corners in the suggestion of a smile, it will be found very often that there is a lessening of tension and an increase in the feeling of well being. Sometimes the feeling of smiling or the slight half smile will be enough to dissipate gloomy or even slightly bitter feelings.

Walking zazen. At the Montreal Zen Centre we sit for periods of thirty-five minutes and after this there is walking zazen, in Japanese *kinhin*. Walking zazen is something of a misnomer as *za* means sitting. However, zazen has become in the West a generic term for all kinds of spiritual practice and so walking zazen has come to be a respectable term. In some countries walking zazen is used as a basic practice. For example, in some monasteries in Sri Lanka it may form the major practice, with sitting zazen being a secondary practice. There is also a difference in the way the Soto and Rinzai (the two different Zen schools of Japan) practice kinhin. The Soto take very small steps, scarcely the length of a foot, and so move very slowly around the *zendo,* the zen practice area. The Rinzai walk at a much more vigorous pace. I was taught to walk at a normal pace, with the eyes down.

Kinhin can be a very useful practice for tense and restless people who find long periods of sitting unbearable. It is also useful for people who have a hard time staying awake. For the practitioner who has no difficulty with sitting zazen, it is useful in that staying fully alert while walking can be considerably more difficult than stationary zazen.

As mentioned previously, there is no particular virtue in the sitting posture itself. People who are having difficulty in adopting one or other of the lotus postures are not thereby handicapped. If there were indeed a virtue in this sitting posture alone, then, as one Zen master pointed out, all the frogs in the world would be awakened. It happens that most people most of the time can practice zazen more effectively using the postures suggested. However, if none of these postures is helpful, alternatives should be found. Kinhin could well be one such alternative.

Posture. With kinhin it is important, as with zazen, that the head be held up and not allowed to droop. The hands are held with the thumb of the right hand folded into the palm of the right hand and the fingers closed around it as a fist. This is put on the chest, with the fingers close to the chest. The left hand is placed on top of the right hand and the elbows are allowed to find a comfortable natural position. When one becomes accustomed to this posture it will be found that it is far preferable to holding the hands in front of the stomach or allowing them to swing at the sides. It is a posture that lends dignity and poise. However, one does have to become used to it so that one can hold it without feeling self-conscious.

As a rule kinhin is maintained for about five to

ten minutes, after which another round of sitting is begun. It is worth repeating that, although one of the values of kinhin during extended sitting periods is that the legs are rested and some of the tension due to restlessness released, the main value of kinhin is that one has the opportunity to practice zazen in motion.

THE MECHANICS OF ZAZEN

Facing the wall. It is a good idea to sit facing a wall rather than to face inward into the room. This is particularly true if one is sitting with others. The reason for this is simply that a wall is less likely to be distracting than the room's interior, which may have furniture, books, and so on. One sits with the knees about twelve to eighteen inches from the wall, which, if possible, should have a plain, uniform surface. The lighting in the room should not be so bright that there is a glare from the wall, nor should it be so dark that one is lulled to sleep by the dullness. For similar reasons, it is best that the room be kept on the cool side. A warm room is conducive to a sleepy state and as many people, particularly beginners, have to struggle with sleepiness anyway, it is best not to do anything to encourage it.

The tendency to drift into a sleepy state may be a kind of resistance to restlessness, a form of overreaction to the restlessness. It can also be a resistance to ideas or memories that are unpleasant and that seem to be pushing their way into consciousness. Of course, it can result from simple fatigue also. But even when one is very tired, it is possible to do good zazen.

The *kyosaku*. At a Zen center formal periods of sitting are supervised by a monitor. The function of a monitor is partly to ensure that any interruptions or untoward events are taken care of so that practitioners can let go completely of any concerns about their environment. If the lights fade, or an unexpected visitor calls, or one of the participants has particular problem, the monitor takes care of it.

However, if the monitor is experienced and well-trained, his or her function is also to help establish and maintain a taut atmosphere. One of the ways this is done is by using the *kyosaku*. This is a specially made stick, flattened at one end, with which the monitor strikes one of the two large shoulder muscles that lie at either side of the neck. Apart from helping a person to overcome sleepiness, this also has the effect of releasing tension that tends to accumulate in the shoulders and neck during zazen.

Some people question the use of the kyosaku. They ask, "Why use it? Is it not at odds with both the atmosphere of zazen and the spirit of non-violence of Buddhism?" This type of objection is made by people who confuse zazen with relaxation techniques. One does not practice Zen to relax, but to discover one's basic relaxed and tranquil state. To relax means that one tries to let go of tension; the word "try" is used because, in the face of tension, this is often all that one can do. It is a bit like covering a bad smell with a sweet perfume, which is all right until the two mix, creating an even worse smell. To try to relax is a contradiction in terms. To find our natural tranquil and relaxed state means that initially we must come to terms with our tension.

Tensions will often surface in the practice of Zen and most frequently they will settle in the shoulders and neck. As we have said, the kyosaku is useful in working with these tensions, in the same way that massage is useful. The kyosaku is also useful in helping people overcome sleepiness. This help is particularly necessary during evening sittings or during long retreats. Another reason for using the kyosaku is that it often happens that some thought or another becomes fixed in the mind; for example, a thought about some wrong, real or imagined, that someone has inflicted upon us. The sudden shock of the kyosaku can usually release us from these thoughts. Finally, and most important, in the hands of a skilled and compassionate monitor, the kyosaku can call up deep latent energies that can then be used in the practice.

In a center that has any claim to be part of an authentic Zen tradition, the kyosaku is used with definite safeguards. In the first place, it is used only by people who have been especially selected and trained and these are normally people who have been practicing Zen for a long time. Furthermore, ritual bowing takes place before the kyosaku is picked up and after each time it is used. This helps maintain awareness or mindfulness in the person using the kyosaku. The kyosaku is never, in such a center, used as an expression of anger and its use has no connotation of punishment or even admonition.

6

Zen in Everyday Life

ZAZEN AS AN END AND AS A MEANS

The need for alert and vital practice becomes obvious once it is realized that in the practice of Zen, zazen is both an end and a means. The seated posture with the hands held in the appropriate position, head up, eyelids lowered, the mind aroused but not resting upon anything—this is a perfect expression of the unity that underlies all, that manifests itself in all. Zazen, however, is also a means and it is this aspect that interests us here.

The practice of Zen shows us the way to pure awareness, awareness that is always present, even in sleep. Normally we are immersed in the activity of the day and totally identified with all that is happening around us. We actively seek this identification because we mistakenly believe that through being totally involved in life we acquire unity or harmony. Identification, we believe, is a way out of the conflicts and feelings of alienation and separation that plague us. Indeed, during the time that we are totally caught up in the doings of our day-to-day existence, we do get some relief. This is the psychological mechanism underlying workaholism. Under the pressure of work, particularly if it is both interesting and demanding, all other problems—a collapsing marriage, financial difficulties, health problems—are temporarily forgotten. The deeper angst of meaninglessness and bewilderment is transmuted into the drive to accomplish, to compete and triumph over others.

However, the unity that is brought on by this is illusory; far from healing our conflicts, we simply submerge them under a flow of energy, enthusiasm, and effort. Moreover, this very effort can act as an additional irritant, creating new conflicts and deepening those that already exist. This calls for new effort, more energy, and results in deeper rifts—we get the feeling of being on a treadmill.

MINDFULNESS AT ALL TIMES

In Zen it is said that the mind must be aroused without resting on anything. Another name for this aroused mental state is mindfulness. After one has practiced seated Zen, it becomes possible to be mindful during the day. With this mindfulness our lives begin to be transformed at a very deep level.

Unfortunately many people misunderstand what this mindfulness means, thinking that it is something like self-observation. Mindfulness for such people then becomes an attempt to blend action and awareness; they try to become more aware of their actions. For example, if they are washing dishes, they try to become more aware of washing the dishes, more aware of the actions of their hands and so on. This self-observation, however, is quite contrary to the development of clear attention, simple awareness. It is, rather, a form of awareness of something "outside" awareness, something separate (the object of awareness can be awareness itself). This simply exacerbates our condition. As can identification, self-observation can provide an illusion of unity, but ultimately serves only to increase our sense of separation. With this increased sense of separation can come a feeling of desperation, even panic, and once again a vicious cycle is set in motion in which desperation engendering deep anxiety and fear is dealt with by "becoming aware of it," by "observing it." This, in turn, increases the sense of separation, out of which the desperation originally came.

This kind of problem arises because people try to take an active part in the development of their awareness. In that, as we have said, this awareness is the basis of all, including all actions, this cannot be done. A Tibetan master said that trying to mix awareness and action is like trying to mix oil and water. It is like trying to step outside one's own skin. Instead, one should notice that during the day there are certain moments when one "surfaces," when one is less immersed, less asleep. If we assent to these moments without necessarily trying to prolong them, they become more and more frequent. In addition, there are moments when we try to get away from situations and ourselves. These are moments of pain and humiliation. If, instead of resisting, we remain quiet and still, while alert, we will find that there will be moments of surfacing even in the darkest experiences.

To be able to accomplish this assenting to moments of awareness, it is necessary that we have fully accepted the first truth of Buddhism: that life is founded upon suffering, that we cannot escape or evade suffering, and that all we can do is to suffer intentionally or unintentionally. Assenting to moments of awareness even during times of great joy is a way of suffering intentionally. This sounds paradoxical until one reflects upon the fact that even joy is transitory and thus can underline, in a very poignant way, the truth that everything is impermanent.

Mindfulness is not an action but an attitude based upon a truth. The attitude is made possible by the faith that we can indeed awaken, that waking sleep is not our true nature. The truth is that we are already awakened; pure awareness is our natural state. A new cycle can be established because this faith is able to make moments of assent possible, and these moments of assent reinforce our faith, while the fundamental truth shines through ever more steadily. Therefore, it cannot be overstressed that there is a basic difference between having faith in awakening and trying to make the awakening happen.

MISTAKEN BELIEFS

Changing the environment. One mistaken belief commonly held is that our inner work would be better or more easily accomplished by abandoning the life that we are leading at the moment and going elsewhere. The rationale for this is almost invariably that the present environment is too confusing, too painful, or too distracting. We assume that if we could go somewhere quiet and less in conflict with the basic need to awaken, it would be possible to work harder and attain better results.

However, there are two errors in this way of thinking. The first we have already discussed: this is the error of believing that in the practice of Zen we are seeking to pacify the mind. The second error stems from the belief that the confusion we experience has its origin in the world rather than in our own attitudes. The problems and confusions of life that surround us have accumulated because of what we are. If we are surrounded by enemies, it is because we *need* enemies; if we are surrounded by debts, it is because we *need* debts, and so on. It may sound strange, but it is nevertheless so. An enemy is one upon whom we have projected our own negative emotions. In the extreme, our enemy is a scapegoat, someone upon whom we have, individually or as a group, projected our pain and so have found some relief. If we have a lot of pain, we need a lot of enemies. If we have little pain, we do not regard even those who try to harm us by calling us names, blaming us, or condemning us as enemies.

If we have inordinate needs, more needs than can be satisfied from our compensation for the work we do, then we borrow and get into debt. Our problem is not so much the debt, or our creditors who insist upon such unpleasant terms to carry the debt, but our own needs. To run away from the debts or the creditors is of little use because in running we carry our needs with us, which will take root in the new environment under one guise or another.

Some of us are dependent upon others, wanting others to support us, look after us, and help us make decisions. With this dependency comes a deep resentment toward those upon whom we are dependent—a resentment that stems from a feeling of being put upon or a belief that these others are trying to take over and control. Once again, it is useless to withdraw from such an environment, believing that somewhere else there will be greater freedom, fewer restrictions imposed by others, or less guilt from being unable to meet the expectations of others. Our need to be dependent on others will manifest itself in the new environment and the same old relationships will be established.

Thus it can be shown, through one example after another, that we are the cause of our own confusion and suffering—that these in the end derive from our own needs. Moreover, these needs are often in conflict with each other, so that the satisfaction of one means the denial of another. For example, one fundamental need is to be unique, to be the center of attention—it might be said that the most popular game of the cosmos is "look at me." Another equally basic need is to belong to a group, to be part of a cause—to lose ourselves in a greater whole. These two needs often conflict and one has to be sacrificed in order that the other may be satisfied. For the pain that results, we blame our environment, fate, or the unfairness of life.

To leave a situation that is painful and confusing in order to be able to work upon oneself more effectively and to be able to meditate more deeply is therefore a mistake. Our confused situation has taken years to develop. When we move to another place there may initially be a lessening of our problems or confusion, because we have not yet put down the roots of our needs. For some time we can live with a false sense of well-being, but after a while, be it months or years, we will find ourselves back in the same pattern, with the same confusion and, with respect to working on ourselves, the intervening months or years will have been wasted.

This does not mean that we have to put up with impossible situations, unworkable marriages, and so on. What it does mean is that we should not move "because it will be helpful to my practice," or because "these difficulties are an obstruction to my practice." Chances are that the very difficulties that we are experiencing are those that can teach us the most.

Changing ourselves. Closely allied to the misconception about changing environments is another: that we must change ourselves. Some of us are convinced that we are unpleasant people—perhaps too hostile or even too timid. Others feel guilty due to some past sins, for which they must atone by becoming different people in the future. Still others feel they must overcome laziness. Most of us share the belief that something about ourselves is wrong that must be put right, and that this putting right can be accomplished either by getting rid of the offending trait—as though it could be plucked out and flung to the winds—or by doing the opposite of what we have been doing for years.

This misconception is often reinforced by people who are ever ready, indeed eager, to point out what is wrong with with us and what we should do to correct our faults. Sometimes they are well-meaning, but most often it is because their relationship with us is painful to themselves and they see getting us to change as a way relieving their pain.

There are now even many companies that encourage managers to discuss the shortcomings of their employees with the employees concerned, to tell them what is "wrong" with their personalities and what they must do to put themselves right. This conjures up the comical picture of one man being told his faults by his boss, the latter in turn having just been told his faults by *his* boss and so on up the line. No doubt many will be pointing out faults identical to those they themselves have been accused of having, even using identical words to do so. This "I'll-tell-you-what-is-wrong-so-that-you-can-put-it-right" attitude is endemic to a society that, being so heavily machine-oriented, has total faith in the interchangeability of parts, provided those parts are standard or "normal." This faith has given birth to the myth of interchangeability of behavioral parts—the standardization of behavior and personality.

However, the notion that we can make up our minds to change ourselves for the better by getting rid of this or that undesirable trait is suspect. This does not mean that we cannot change for the better—it simply means that we may not be able to select beforehand those aspects that we consider undesirable and then start eliminating them. The personality of a person is like a landscape, with hills and valleys, bogs and meadows, marshlands and gardens. It is an ecological whole; to change one part means that all are changed, for each part is interdependent with all the others. To use another metaphor, each person has his or her own light and along with that light goes a shadow. To eliminate the shadow we must put out the light.

This reasoning might be seen as pessimistic but, as mentioned earlier, pessimism is not the same as facing up to unpleasant truths, but rather dwelling on the unpleasantness and overlooking the truth. In fact, this reasoning is very optimistic, very liberating, for if we cannot change ourselves purposely, then we are relieved of the tremendous burden of having to do so. If there are no evil demons, we do not have to waste a lot of time, effort, and resources to appease those demons.

Some may object to what is being said on the grounds that it might lead people to act irresponsibly, not caring about the effect that their actions have on others. This is an important objection, one that cannot be easily dismissed, but unfortunately it also relates to too many issues to deal with adequately in an introductory book. However, let me say that the objection implies that ethical conduct and concern for others are only possible if we are able to consciously change ourselves. But perhaps responsibility, ethical conduct, concern for others, etc., do not derive from this at all, but rather from realizing the truth that we are all one, and that this unity or oneness is the ground of all being. Our problems arise because we try to invest this oneness with specific qualities; we strive to be good, to be loving, to be holy, and so on, and instead of attaining oneness we acquire some quality, which is set against all other qualities and so separates us from others and divides us irrevocably. We lose touch with what we really are and become alienated and confused. In ancient China a provincial governor once went to a temple for a retreat. When he was leaving, the Zen master asked him, "How are you going to rule the people?" The governor replied, "With wisdom and compassion." "Then," retorted the master, "every last one will suffer!"

Does this mean that we are irrevocably locked in our prison of personality, that anything goes?

Not at all. The very basis of Buddhist practice is liberation, but it is liberation from the tyranny of "good and bad," "right and wrong," "popular and unpopular," "likable and unlikable," those antitheses over which so much argument has been expended and so many wars have been fought. This liberation is true freedom. To be required to totally free ourselves from our "bad" aspects, our "evil" aspects, in order to live with the good of ourselves—this would be eternal bondage.

When we practice Zen we do not sit with the intention of getting rid of our restlessness or anxiety, nor do we try to improve ourselves by becoming like the model that our parents, wives, friends, or even teachers hold up for us. In fact, a teacher who tries to get us to change, even if it is "for our own good," is not a true Zen teacher. To accept ourselves just as we are, with all our faults intact, with all our shortcomings and inadequacies, and to do so without putting the blame on our parents or the way we were brought up, without resenting people for abusing us or wronging us, and without projecting a better, more loving, or more caring self in the future, is *very* painful. It is so painful in fact that we can usually remain this way only for brief spells before retreating into a fog of thoughts and ideas.

But we must return to this pain again and again. To sit with a clear mind is to drop the fog and with it our justifications and excuses for being bad, our resolutions and promises to be good. And with this clarity comes the lash of contradictions inherent in us all. When this becomes too violent we seek to escape—escape again to the belief that we can and will change. This is why zazen is difficult. Indeed, to practice zazen is not to abandon the ethics of religion but to live those ethics fully in a natural, spontaneous way. If we cannot do this then we still have a long way to go with our practice.

THE INNER MONOLOGUE

The inner monologue is our natural response to these internal clashes and contradictions. All through the day something like a private soap opera is going on in our minds. The scenario is disjointed and confused, moving in no fixed direction. Sometimes the drama takes place in the foreground, sometimes in the background of our minds. Should someone stand on our corns he or she immediately becomes the villain of the piece, but for the most part the scenario is wearily, boringly the same.

When we are mindful, however, we cut through this clutter; when the mind is aroused without resting on anything the monologue dries up. It is not a question of seeking to suppress the monologue; one does not try actively to banish it. However, some activities can only take place in the dark and this monologue is one of them. In the light of awareness the steady drain of energies ceases as the ghosts of the mind vanish. It is like a classroom from which the teacher is absent. The children make a lot of noise, throw things, pull one another's hair, and jump around—all to let off energy. When the teacher returns, he or she will not try to restore order by shouting and hitting; this would simply add to the noise. The wise teacher instead simply stands there; one by one the children will slide into their seats and silence will reign. But to just stand there, that is the difficulty.

THE WAY OF THE WARRIOR

It is said that Zen is the "way of the warrior"; this is so for several reasons. A warrior advancing on his adversary is alert but not tense. His alertness is like that of a cat sitting outside the hole of a mouse—flexible, fluid, not braced for the worst nor tense with anticipation. Such a cat may almost seem sleepy, but let the mouse show a whisker and bang!—it's all over. When one sits in zazen, one sits with the alertness of a warrior, free of entangling thoughts and emotions. If a warrior is distracted by worry, fear, even a stray thought, his adversary has a gap through which to attack and the warrior will lose his life. So it is with zazen: if we lose clear attention—our flexible awareness—even for an instant, we are quickly drowned in a flood of thoughts and lose our precious life of oneness.

The way of Zen is also called the way of the warrior because both ways require courage. As mentioned earlier, the thoughts, the monologue with its scenario, is a screen—like a smoke screen—used to hide our pain, humiliation, and restlessness from ourselves. When the smoke clears, we can no longer avoid the total discomfort of our situation. It takes courage to allow the smoke to clear. Nevertheless, just as the dull dross of the *massa confusa*, the confused mass, is transmuted into gold by the alchemist, so it is out of the pain of contradiction and confusion that our awareness is released. As the sun of awareness rises, more and more of the dark shapes that inhabit our twilight world vanish as specters. More and more we see that our lives are filled with tragedies, accidents, calamities that never really happened. More and more we realize, as did the great Zen master Nansen, that our everyday life is the Way. By learning how to suffer, we have the power not to suffer.

This realization enables us to understand why it is said on the one hand that there is nothing we have to do, that all striving simply adds to our confusion; and yet all the patriarchs and masters, beginning with Buddha himself, have stressed the need for effort. Zen master Dogen says that it takes tears, sweat, and sometimes blood. Yasutani Roshi used to say that just to sit will cause us to perspire.

Striving to change ourselves would appear to be a waste of effort. No matter how valiant the striving, we simply bang one dent out by banging another dent in. However, we cannot help trying to ameliorate the suffering our condition brings with it; striving to change is one of the ways that we attempt this amelioration, and is therefore in accord with the flow of life. But to come to awakening is to go against this flow and open ourselves to the pain. We have to swim against the current of thoughts, judgments, and ideas that are designed both to seal up the gaps in our armor and to dissipate the energy that the pain engenders.

A favorite image in Zen temples is the carp. To spawn, a carp must swim upstream, against the current, through rapids, and even over waterfalls. The leaps must be done using the power of the total body. Time and again a leap is made, only to have the rush of water carry the fish downstream once more. This effort of the carp is symbolic of the effort, perseverance, and determination to continue that is needed in the practice of Zen. However, it is an effort of an entirely new kind compared with the efforts that we normally make to assuage the pain associated with the projects, competitions, and goals of our daily life. It is an effortless effort, an effort not to be swept away by the flood of habitual efforts. It is an effort simply to arouse the mind.

To think about this, to reason about it, is impossible and simply leads one into contradictions and paradoxes. Only in the exerting of the effort to maintain an alert, interested, and flexible mind, independent of thought, form, and words, does the nature and reality of the difficulty involved, as well as the impossibility of describing what is necessary, become apparent. Let me say again—it is not an effort to stop the flow, to empty the mind, to cease thinking that is called for; it is the effort to arouse the mind without resting it upon anything. Because of the difficulties involved, and the need for support, encouragement, and guidance, most people find it easier to work with a group and to have someone alongside as a guide.

7

Practice at a Center

THE IMPORTANCE OF GUIDANCE

In most large towns nowadays there is at least one Buddhist group, and sometimes several—Zen, Tibetan, Vipassana, Pure Land—and most people who practice Buddhism seriously do so with a group. This, of course, does not mean they do not also practice on their own. On the contrary, individual practice is both rewarding and important. However, it is usually supplemented and complemented by working with others.

There are two major problems to be overcome if one is to carry on a Zen practice: the first is to get to the cushion, and the second is to stay there. By maintaining a regular schedule of attendance at a center, the first can be overcome; by working with others and adopting the discipline of the group, the second can be overcome. This, in turn, will enable one to get much deeper into the practice. Few people are able to commit themselves totally to anything; there is always some part of themselves that is left out and that nags, criticizes, or looks desperately around for alternatives. When one practices with a group, there is less likelihood of this problem becoming serious enough to interrupt the practice. To some extent the conflict abates and energy that is normally used in struggling with alternatives can be applied to practice.

It can be readily appreciated that if one is to come to awakening, it is likely that long and hard work will need to be done. Such work, furthermore, is foreign to the general disposition of people in the West today, where a great emphasis is placed upon entertainment, novelty, and distraction. However, it is also clear that awakening has been sought after in all spiritual traditions—although it is not always known by this name—and it is an unconscious search for this awakening that gives rise to the deep yearning and unrest that most people experience at different times in their lives.

Having said this, it is well to bear in mind the admonition of the masters and patriarchs that we not set up spiritual goals, nor consciously strive to attain or realize them, for this will simply block true practice. It is better to regard practice as a gift to life, a giving of oneself to what one could call the life-force or Buddha nature. Most religions have personified this force: as Christ, Krishna, Buddha, and so on. Such personification has the advantage of making the practice and gift warmer and more concrete. The term "life-force" is somewhat cold and abstract and, to some extent, misleading. However, a disadvantage of the personification is that it can be an invitation to the imagination to weave all kinds of images, stories, myths, and theories that can take on their own reality and block all spiritual development. With or without personification, practice is still a long and arduous task. Therefore, it is good to have companions along the way, friends who will give support when the going gets difficult and one begins to forget what the journey is all about.

The importance of a teacher. All true ways insist upon the need for a teacher. There are many blind alleys, false trails, and places where the path peters out completely. If there is no one to give guidance at these times, months or even years of work can be wasted. But it is essential that this guide has traveled the way already and can, in fact, act as a true guide. The dangers inherent in the blind leading the blind are as great in Zen as in any other endeavor, and the fact that a person calls himself or herself a Zen teacher is no guarantee of insight or ability. What is most important is that the teacher has come to awakening and that this awakening has been authenticated by a competent teacher whose own awakening was, in turn, verified. No person can help another to awakening, no matter how well intentioned, well-meaning, and well-versed in all aspects of Zen, if that person has not himself or herself come to true awakening. It is necessary that the awakening be authenticated because during practice one experiences many moments that can be quite striking, moments of deep psychological and philosophical insight or profound visions and realizations, all of which are inspiring and rewarding, but none of which is awakening. It is impossible to describe awakening—indeed one of its hallmarks is that it is beyond description and expression. However, an awakened person can tell whether another has come to awakening, and, to some extent, the depth of that awakening. Moreover, awakening by itself is not enough; integration of awakening into everyday life is also necessary, and for most this will take from ten to fifteen years.

Furthermore, if one is to be a teacher for Westerners, considerable life experience is necessary. Zen practice in the East was, and still is, primarily monastic. Life in a monastery, although by no means easy or even tranquil, is nevertheless very simple compared to lay life. The modern lay practitioner usually marries, brings up a family, pursues a career, has social obligations, etc., and therefore unquestionably lives a more complex and, perhaps, a more demanding life than an ordained person living in a monastery. A teacher who has not personally negotiated the reefs and shoals of lay life may not be able to conceive of the difficulties involved, and certainly cannot stand as any kind of living inspiration.

All of these contribute to one of the difficulties that Zen practitioners in the West face—an acute shortage of adequately trained teachers. And this situation in turn means that there is a great risk that the vacuum will be filled by people with inadequate qualifications and who will likely cause a great deal of confusion. One might think that for those who simply want to meditate and who have no aspirations to awakening, a shortage of teachers would not be a problem. However, anything that is effective is at the same time and to the same degree hazardous. To say that one is not worried about whether or not a teacher is qualified is somewhat like saying that one believes meditation has power neither to heal nor to harm. This is dangerously naive. There are several good books on the hazards of spiritual work, some of which should be required reading for anyone interested in the new spiritual ways.[1]

[1]See in particular *Snapping*, by Flo Conway and Jim Siegelman (New York: Delta Books, 1978) and *Cults of Unreason*, by Dr. Christopher Evans (New York: Delta Books, 1973).

LIFE AT A CENTER

In order to provide some insight into what a center is like, I shall talk about the Montreal Zen Centre. This is not to say that this is the only or even the best way a center should operate. However, most centers are fairly similar to it. The Montreal Centre is an offshoot of the Rochester Zen Center, which is directed by Roshi Philip Kapleau, author of the *Three Pillars of Zen* and other books. The Rochester Center in turn is modeled on Hoshinji Zen Monastery of Japan, which in its heyday was under the direction of Harada Roshi and was considered to be one of the more dynamic monasteries in Japan. Harada Roshi and one of his chief disciples, Yasutani Roshi, were two of the teachers Roshi Kapleau worked with during his thirteen years in Japan. Harada Roshi was originally a Soto Zen Buddhist, but later worked with a Rinzai master and came to awakening under his direction. Yasutani also, before working with Harada Roshi, was a Soto teacher. They are both remarkable in that they started as Soto priests and came to awakening under Rinzai masters. This is said to be remarkable because, as is the way with human beings, Zen practice in Japan has polarized into two distinct groups or sects: Rinzai and Soto. For someone to span both sects and to see that each has its advantages and disadvantages requires considerable courage and openness of mind.

Montreal Zen Centre is a lay community, but it has a residential program as well as non-residential membership. Residents pursue their own vocations and careers, but live as a spiritual family. The basis of the program is spiritual and only people who have a serious commitment to practice are accepted. This commitment includes willingness to attend most of the activities of the center, as well as the determination to struggle to live harmoniously with others. Building on a spiritual foundation, this proves much easier than would otherwise be the case, and one of the features of this and other Zen communities is the depth of harmony attained. The lifestyle is fairly austere; for example, there is no smoking or drinking in the house—indeed, no resident has so far been inclined toward either of these habits. There is no TV and hi-fi music is played quietly. Food is normally prepared and eaten communally; it is vegetarian and, although skillfully cooked, it might be considered plain to the taste of many.

A typical day begins at 5:30 a.m. with a wake-up bell and from 5:45 to 7:15 a.m. there is zazen followed by chanting (about which more will be said later). After the chanting, residents change and prepare for breakfast. More chanting takes place before and after food is served, although while food is being served silence is maintained.

But after the chanting the atmosphere is relaxed and there is usually lively talk. Experiments were made with residents having breakfast independently, but it was found that the harmony of the house suffered; there is a lot more to eating together than simply satisfying the appetite. After breakfast, some residents prepare for work while those who have time clear the table and wash the dishes.

On several evenings each week members who live outside the center come for zazen. These sessions start at 7:30 p.m. and go on until 9:30 p.m. The two hours are divided into three thirty-five-minute periods of zazen, with kinhin in between. The evening ends with chanting and prostrations. Anyone can be a member of the center who wishes to join, provided they also practice at home. There is no insistence that one give up another religion to be a member, and encouragement is given to people who have a practice derived from another tradition, provided that it is authentic and not likely to disturb other members.

Although a center is a non-profit organization, a monthly fee is charged in order that the costs of the mortgage, utilities, and so on can be met. No one in particular benefits from these contributions; they are all used for the community as a whole. However, even these regular monthly contributions are generally insufficient for the sup-

port of a center and it has to rely also upon dona-
tions from those able to make them.

THE DISCIPLINE OF SESSHIN

Once each month, except for July and August, a
sesshin is held lasting four days or seven days.
This Japanese word means roughly "one mind"
and is the occasion for a number of people to join
together for an intense period of zazen, a kind of
retreat. The daily schedule for sesshin is given on
page 125. Silence is maintained throughout the
sesshin and participants are also asked to keep
their eyes down at all times. This helps to develop
an intense atmosphere, which, in turn, makes it
easier for the participants to get deeply into their
practice. To some people this kind of discipline
sounds difficult, but most who actually undertake
it find relief in being able to let go of the burden
that conversation, discussion, and argument impose, and after completing one sesshin are ready
to attend another. Sesshin has been called a
spiritual spring-cleaning. It is very difficult to
describe the effect it has upon one, other than to
say that even for beginners sesshin gives at least a
glimpse of what life could be like if we could live
from a clear mind.

Apart from zazen and kinhin, during sesshin
there are work periods, talks by and private encounters with the teacher, and chanting. The

work period is very important, not only to accomplish the cleaning, cooking, and maintenance that is necessary during sesshin, but to encourage awareness while moving around and working. The talks that are given to sesshin participants are of two types. One is an encouragement talk. The other, called *teisho*, is more difficult to describe, as it is a cross between a lecture and an encouragement talk. Encouragement talks help participants maintain the intense vigilance required by Zen practice. This vigilance can wane under the weight of the long hours of zazen and encouragement can help restore the required faith and energy. Teisho does not aim at simply informing or instructing, but is an encouragement to awaken the mind. A good teacher will speak from his or her own awakened state and in so doing transmit this awakened state on a non-verbal level.

The private encounter with the teacher can also be of two kinds. Beginning participants will take problems concerning posture, anxieties, pains, uncontrollable thoughts, and so on to this encounter. More experienced participants will seek clarification of points of Buddhist doctrine. Both types of encounter take the form of a counseling session. But later, and often mixed with this counseling, will emerge a new kind of encounter in which there is a mutual testing. This is not a type of conflict, but a way through which the practitioner tries to see into the truth, or plumb the depths, and the teacher will do all in her or his power to assist. This kind of encounter has been likened to a chick that, when it is ready, begins to peck from inside the egg, while the hen in turn pecks from outside.

TYPICAL SCHEDULE FOR SESSHIN

First day

6:30 p.m.	Zendo open for informal sitting.
7:00 p.m.	Zazen begins
9:30 p.m.	End of formal sitting
10:00 p.m.	Tea available in kitchen

Following days

4:30 a.m.	Wake-up
5:00 a.m.	Zazen
7:00 a.m.	Breakfast
7:20 a.m.	Work period
8:30 a.m.	Rest period
9:30 a.m.	Zazen
10:10 a.m.	Teisho
11:15 a.m.	Zazen
12:30 p.m.	Lunch and break
1:30 p.m.	Zazen
3:30 p.m.	Chanting
3:50 p.m.	Exercise

SCHEDULE FOR SESSHIN *(cont.)*

Following days

4:30 p.m.	Zazen
5:00 p.m.	Supper
5:25 p.m.	Rest period
7:00 p.m.	Zazen
9:30 p.m.	End of formal sitting
10:00 p.m.	Tea available in kitchen

Last day

1:15 p.m.	Zazen
3:15 p.m.	Closing words and chanting
3:45 p.m.	Work period
4:30 p.m.	Supper

Note: Private instruction is offered in the afternoon and evening periods for those who desire it.

KOAN PRACTICE

To help deepen practice and to assist in the interchange during private encounters with practitioners, a teacher of the Rinzai tradition will assign a *koan*, which is a saying, or sometimes a doing, of a Zen master or of Buddha (as, for example, the well-known conundrum "What is the sound of one hand clapping?"). This practice is followed, when appropriate, at the Montreal Zen Centre.

When a Zen master speaks, he or she does so from that which underlies all opposites, or from that out of which all opposites emerge. To comprehend what such a highly developed person means, one must likewise let go of the normal dualistic disposition of the mind. The logical impasse created by the seemingly irrational, unsolvable koan helps free the mind from its ordinary conceptual framework and allows one to see directly into reality-as-is. To successfully accomplish this is awakening, and it is the struggle to turn the mind away from its habitual dualistic mode that gives rise to the intense struggle that is necessary in Zen practice.

Because the teacher has already worked with the koan, a special kind of relationship is able to develop in which the koan is the bridge, while the results of the practitioner's work is that which crosses over the bridge. It is therefore unwise for someone to work alone on a koan. In the first place, because there is no one who can make the koan alive, this solitary practice is a waste of time. In addition, a koan has the power to pinpoint and crystallize some very basic psychological concerns, and there is the possibility that those concerns may find their way into consciousness in the form of intense anxiety and dread. If no competent help is available, this can give rise to some very difficult moments indeed.

MAKYO

A major barrier to awakening in Zen practice is called *makyo*. Again, a Japanese word is used because there is no satisfactory English equivalent. Generally speaking, all that arises in practice short of awakening is called makyo; it can therefore include ecstatic states as well as fearful ones. The nearest English description would be "illusory" or even "delusory," but somehow the first term is misleading and the second too ominous. There is no doubt that the fear that one sometimes feels in Zen practice is real, not illusory, and yet it is makyo. Likewise, one will sometimes experience a beauteous state in which the mind, body, and world are all merged in a condition of quiet joy and release. This too is very real, but it is still makyo. At other times, one knows in advance what another is going to say, for example, one's teacher during an encouragement talk, or even in a private encounter. At such times it seems that an outer layer has somehow been peeled away from reality and one is participating directly with other minds. This too is makyo.

Many religions set great store by these special experiences, but in Zen they are, if dwelt upon and accorded special value, only an impediment. One great Zen master said words to the effect that his great magic and miraculous powers were chopping wood and drawing water from the well.

A modern master might say, "my great magic and miraculous powers are washing dishes and putting out the garbage." In other words, the miracle is not that one might be able to walk on water but that one can walk at all.

Probably the most familiar and frequent makyo experience is psychological insight. Sometimes the whole mental structure will undergo a substantial shift of center; old traumas are resolved or released, and with this previously fixed considerations and judgments are let go of. Particularly for one with an intellectual disposition, these shifts can be precious. If they are deep enough they can even bring about a complete reorientation of one's whole view of life and the world; consequently they are often confused with awakening. Again, there is no question about the reality of such mental shifts—indeed reality itself can sometimes be reappraised and re-evaluated because of them. Nevertheless, they are still makyo, and a good teacher, without ignoring or dismissing them, will take steps to guide the practitioner back to the practice. Unless this is done, the mind of the practitioner might explode into a flurry of thoughts, assessments, and ideas like a hive of bees that has been disturbed.

Equally difficult to deal with are fear and dread, which can come suddenly and unannounced. One of the causes of this is, paradoxically, tensions giving way and shifts taking place in what might be called our "kinesthetic awareness." We all have a *sensation* of ourselves. This sensation includes tensions as well as other kinds of sensations—those arising from crossing the legs or folding the arms, rubbing the nose or the back of the head. Through awareness of these sensations we maintain a "standard" sense of ourselves. In situations that are confused or uncertain, the need to hold on to this sensation of ourselves increases. Tensions mount and we seek relief through a set of sensation rituals, means by which we are able to maintain our sense of being.

This sensation of ourselves might be described as a cathedral of tensions, because, as in the case of Gothic cathedrals, each tension holds all the other tensions in place. During deep zazen then, a basic tension can give way, altering the whole structure, bringing about a change in our kinesthetic awareness. We have the feeling that a fundamental shift has taken place in what until now we have considered our being, ourselves. We feel as though for the moment we have lost contact with ourselves, a feeling accompanied by a total loss of our sense of direction. This can generate a considerable amount of anxiety while it is happening and, if one does not understand what is going on, the anxiety coupled with the kinesthetic shift can bring about a damaging loss of confidence. This can have psychological repercussions lasting weeks and even months.

The kinesthetic shift is, of course, only one of the causes for fear and anxiety arising in practice and is another form of makyo. However, if these fears are not held on to, the consequences of such an experience can be considerable realignment—for the good—of one's whole perspective and perhaps even insight into the nature of the kinesthetic sense itself. A good teacher will have experienced this and other fears in his or her own practice and will have no trouble in offering reassurance. There is also a general maxim that should be borne in mind: Whatever is caused by zazen will be resolved by zazen, and the resolution almost always is in the direction of greater stability and insight. However, it is wise to talk over such problems with an experienced teacher.

CHANTING

Finally, a word about chanting, which plays an important but not large part in sesshin. Examples of some of the chants are given below. During sesshin, chanting is done for about twenty minutes each afternoon, as well as before meals and at the close of the day's formal activities. However, although chanting does not take up any substantial portion of sesshin time, the chants do represent a vital part of Zen practice—particularly *The Four Vows*—so it would be wise to spend some time discussing them.

The Prajna Paramita Hridaya Sutra

The Bodhisattva of Compassion
from the depths of prajna wisdom
saw the emptiness of all five
skandhas and sundered the bonds
that caused him suffering.

Know then:
Form here is only emptiness,
emptiness only form.
Form is no other than emptiness,
emptiness no other than form.

Feeling, thought, and choice,
consciousness itself,
are the same as this.

Dharmas here are empty,
all are the primal void.
None are born or die.
Nor are they stained or pure,
nor do they wax or wane.

So in emptiness no form,
no feeling, thought, or choice,
nor is there consciousness.

No eye, ear, nose,
tongue, body, mind;
no color, sound, smell,

taste, touch, or what
the mind takes hold of,
nor even act of sensing.

No ignorance or end of it
nor all that comes of ignorance:
no withering, no death,
no end of them.

Nor is there pain or cause of pain
or cease in pain or noble path
to lead from pain,
not even wisdom to attain,
attainment too is emptiness.

So know that the Bodhisattva
holding to nothing whatever
but dwelling in prajna wisdom
is freed of delusive hindrance,
rid of the fear bred by it,
and reaches clearest nirvana.

All Buddhas of past and present,
Buddhas of future time
through faith in prajna wisdom
come to full enlightenment.

Know then the great dharani
the radiant, peerless mantra,
the supreme, unfailing mantra,

the *Prajna Paramita,*
whose words allay all pain.
This is highest wisdom
true beyond all doubt,
know and proclaim its truth:

> Gate, gate,
> paragate,
> parasamgate,
> bodhi, svaha!

Prajna paramita is at the heart of the teaching of
Zen. *Prajna* is the Sanskrit term for the simple
awareness without reflection that is Zen contemplation, discussed in Chapter 4; *paramita*
means "to cross to the other side"; *hridaya* means
"the heart." *The Prajna Paramita Hridaya Sutra* is
a religious text that extols prajna as the way
beyond duality and therefore the way beyond suffering. It is from the depths of awareness—
that is, from the state of *having the mind aroused
without resting upon any form, image, idea, or
thought*—that the bodhisattva sees into the emptiness of the five skandhas, discussed in Chapter 3.

In the same chapter we also discussed the concept of emptiness. The following expression from
the Zen tradition is one of the most sublime of all
spiritual affirmations:

> Form here is only emptiness,
> emptiness only form.

All forms are modification of pure awareness, which itself has no form. As an analogy, consider all wooden things—chairs and tables, planks and blocks of wood, trees of all kinds. These are all forms of wood. But wood without form cannot be apprehended; it is as unknowable as emptiness without form. But note that the unknowability of all implies an ineffectiveness of all thought, knowledge, sensory input, and mental processes—in short, a negation of Buddhist teaching and practice:

> not even wisdom to attain,
> attainment too is emptiness.

Even prajna, even contemplation itself—this too is emptiness. To go beyond even any thought of going beyond, this is prajna paramita. The final lines of the sutra, which are older than Buddhism itself, state:

> Gate, gate,
> paragate,
> parasamgate,
> bodhi, svaha!

This might be translated:

> Gone, gone,
> gone beyond,
> gone quite beyond,
> bodhi, svaha!

Bodhi is the source of the light of knowing, that which is beyond all beyonds. We might say it is the source of simple awareness. It is beyond not in light years of distance nor in eons of time, but it is beyond in the way of being inaccessible to the reflecting mind. A Hindu song sings:

> My Lord is in my eye; that is why I see him everywhere.

Svaha! means rejoice. Who would not rejoice at the slightest stirring of this Mother of all Buddhas, as the *Prajna Paramita* is often referred to?

Ten-Verse Kannon Sutra

Kanzeon!
Praise to Buddha!
All are one with Buddha,
all awake to Buddha.
Buddha, Dharma, Sangha:
freedom, joy, and purity.
Through the day Kanzeon,
through the night Kanzeon.
This thought comes from Buddha-mind.
This thought is one with Buddha-mind.

The protagonist of *The Prajna Paramita Hridaya Sutra* is the Bodhisattva of Compassion. The term bodhisattva has several meanings. It can mean a very highly developed person who forgoes entering nirvana in order to help other beings in need. It can also simply refer to someone who is on the way, someone who has in all earnestness taken *The Four Vows* (page 142). This particular bodhisattva is known in Sanskrit by the name Avalokitesvara, in Japanese by the name Kanzeon (or Kannon). Avalokitesvara was originally a man, a disciple of Buddha, who came to awakening through seeing into the nature of sound. Later, as the devotional aspect of Buddhism became developed, Avalokitesvara was transformed in the popular imagination and iconography into a woman. In this devotional aspect, Kanzeon functions as the Bodhisattva of Compassion. She possesses many attributes strikingly similar to those of the Virgin Mary.

The name of the Bodhisattva of Compassion, Kanzeon, is invoked in the above chant. Just as each sentient being is intrinsically Buddha, each is also intrinsically Kanzeon. As Buddha is the manifestation of our awakened nature, so Kanzeon is the manifestation of the compassionate nature inherent in all of us. The chant is an invocation of this compassion.

Kanzeon is said to have a thousand eyes and a thousand arms; the eyes allow her to see the suffering of the world, the arms allow her to heal. Sometimes she is even depicted as having a number of heads: at the Montreal Centre there is an eleven-headed Kanzeon. This iconography caused early Christian missionaries in the Orient a great deal of difficulty; they determined that Buddhists worshiped monsters. However, now that the sensibilities of the West have been awakened to new views of reality through cubist, impressionist, and surrealist art, we find such portrayals much less startling.

To invoke the compassionate nature is to awaken to the sufferings of others and to arouse the will to work for the salvation of all. Through this endeavor we can gain a new perspective on our own sufferings, which can be seen as part of the unfolding saga of Buddha nature or the *élan vital*.

Hakuin Zenji's Chant in Praise of Zazen

From the beginning all beings are Buddha.
Like water and ice,
without water no ice,
outside us no Buddhas.
How near the truth
yet how far we seek,
like one in water crying "I thirst!"
Like a child of rich birth
wandering poor on this earth,
we endlessly circle the six worlds.
The cause of our sorrow is ego delusion.
From dark path to dark path we've wandered
    in darkness—

How can we be free from the wheel of *samsara?*
The gateway to freedom is zazen *samadhi*—
beyond exaltation, beyond all our praises,
the pure Mahayana.
Observing the precepts, repentance and giving,
the countless good deeds, and the way of right
    living
all come from zazen.
Thus one true *samadhi* extinguishes evils;
it purifies karma, dissolving obstructions.
Then where are the dark paths to lead us astray?
The pure lotus land is not far away.
Hearing this truth, heart humble and grateful,
to praise and embrace it, to practice its wisdom,
brings unending blessings, brings mountains
    of merit.
But if we turn inward and prove our True-nature—
that True-self is no-self
our own Self is no-self—
we go beyond ego and past clever words.
Then the gate to the oneness of cause-and-effect
    is thrown open.
Not two and not three, straight ahead
    runs the Way
Our form now being no-form,
in coming and going we never leave home.
Our thought now being no-thought,
our dancing and songs are the voice of the
    Dharma.
How vast is the heaven of boundless *samadhi!*

How bright and transparent the moonlight of
  wisdom!
What is there outside us,
what is there we lack?
Nirvana is openly shown to our eyes.
This earth where we stand is the pure lotus land,
and this very body the body of Buddha.

Hakuin was a seventeenth-century Japanese Zen
master. He was a deeply awakened man and his
teaching helped to inspire a revival of interest in
Zen practice in Japan. His chant has three phases
or stages. The first is the stage of awakening to
our plight, to the realization that, although in-
herently Buddha, nevertheless:

> From dark path to dark path
>   we've wandered in darkness—
> How can we be free from
>   the wheel of *samsara?*

The "wheel of *samsara*" is a Buddhist metaphor
for the suffering in life that is the result of our ignorance. The next stage of the chant extols the
virtue of sitting, which leads to *samadhi*, Sanskrit
for the knowing unity that pervades all. This is
the way of prayer, of meditation, and of concentration that leads to unification—to those rare
moments "beyond exaltation, beyond all our
praises." The following is a description of one
such moment:

Suddenly, and without warning, something invisible seemed to be drawn across the sky, transforming the world about me into a kind of tent of concentrated and enhanced significance. What had been merely an out-side became an inside. The objective was somehow transformed into a completely sub-jective fact, which was experienced as "mine," but on a level where the word had no meaning; for "I" was no longer the familiar ego. Nothing more can be said about the experience.[2]

This practice brings us "unending blessings" and "mountains of merit." But Hakuin's chant goes on to say "if we turn inward and prove our true nature," this is awakening. From this point to the end of the chant Hakuin is referring to the awakened state, a state that does not come and go because it is always present, a state that does not give unending blessings but is the very source of the blessings themselves. This very earth on which we stand is the "pure lotus land" (heaven) and this very body the body of Buddha. Indeed, just as we are and have always been cannot really be described as a state; but to see into what this means is difficult.

[2]From *Mysticism*, by F. C. Happold (New York: Penguin, 1963), p. 130.

The Four Vows

All beings without number,
   I vow to liberate.
Endless blind passions,
   I vow to uproot.
Dharma gates without number,
   I vow to penetrate.
The great way of Buddha,
   I vow to attain.

These vows are not taken in the presence of God or of Buddha or of any other person. They are, instead, an affirmation of a deep longing to come to awakening. All that we human beings do can be seen to be a manifestation of this longing, even though the resultant acts and thoughts are almost always distorted and abortive. The four statements are called vows because they commit us wholly to realize what we long for.

It is important to notice the order of these vows. The first is a vow to come to awakening not for ourselves alone but for all living beings. This is not an altruistic vow, but an intensely practical one that, if taken seriously, helps take the practice out of the realm of mere psychological exercise, undertaken for egoistic reasons, into a transcendent realm in which ego and other are seen as one mind. Indeed, to practice for oneself alone can only end in increased loneliness and alienation. As one's practice matures, the boundary between self and other becomes more permeable; instead of self being one substance and the other another substance, with the two divided by an ubridgeable gap, both are seen to be of one substance. To love others is thus natural; we do not have to learn to love, but instead learn to stop separating ourselves from others.

The second vow is to uproot the passions of greed, anger, and ignorance. In Buddhism it is said that the only sin is ignorance. This may come as a surprise to many people who look upon ignorance as a passive state that cannot be helped. Ignorance, they believe, comes from lack of information, a lack that can be overcome by education. In Buddhism, ignorance is seen to be active; we actively ignore the totality in favor of a part. To uproot the passion of ignorance is to see everything as a whole, complete in itself. Yasutani Roshi used to say, "Every one is a complete meal; even a cracked cup is perfect as a cracked cup." Anger and greed flourish in the darkness of ignorance. We are greedy for that which will nourish and preserve the part that we have selected as all important; we are angry when that part is slighted or threatened. In the sun of awakening the shadows of greed are transformed into the radiance of compassion, while the thickets of anger blossom as the flowers of commitment.

The third vow is the vow to penetrate the furthest gate of dharma, the truth as propounded by Buddha. The great Japanese master Dogen said, "There is no beginning to practice or end of awakening; there is no beginning to awakening or end to practice." We can always go deeper. To rest on the way is human; to stop on the way is impossible. We go either forward or backward. Each encounter we have with some person or some situation, each moment of anger or greed, conflict, or suspicion, success or failure, represents a dharma gate that we either penetrate or close against ourselves.

The last vow—to attain the great way of Buddha—is to realize the great way of awakening to the wholeness and completeness of all. How wonderful that we can even contemplate such a vow, the vow to realize fully what we all are: the spiritual sun that gives life and light to all without exception.

The three prostrations. These vows are chanted three times, mindfully and with full awareness of their implications. Following the three vows three prostrations are made. The vows are an affirmation, an assertion, and it is fitting that they are followed by a gesture of humility, a gesture that humankind has practiced since time immemorial.

The language of the body is unique and personal. It is fascinating to learn its grammar and syntax and to note how our various states of mind, even the most subtle, even those we would so want to hide, have their own related gestures. How many different ways there are of licking the lips, of coughing, of opening, closing, or half-closing the eyes. It has been said that there is a complicated, subliminal dance that accompanies our speech and that each culture has its own dance. It is a moot point whether the dance calls forth the words or the words call forth the dance. Either way, we cannot overlook gesture. The bow and the prostration, these come from the most profound depths of our aliveness.

In the practice of Zen we do not bow to another, but in the face of the "other." It is said that Zen is the way of "self power," and that other religions, for example, Christianity, are the way of "other power." If this means anything, it means that Zen is the way to the other through the self and that other religions are the way to the self through the other. Both lead to unity or holiness, which is beyond self and other. On the Buddhist altar is a figure of Buddha; this is the other. Bowing acknowledges the other, but not as something separate. As long as we see Buddha as something or someone other, we find that what was a window has become a wall. A monk named

Etcho asked a Zen master, "What is Buddha?" The master replied, "You are Etcho."

Methods of chanting. Chanting in Zen is very vital. It is accompanied by the steady beating of a *mokugyo*, a round drum made of wood, and the striking of a *keisu*, a large bowl-shaped gong. On the whole, the chanting is around a monotone and has hara as its origin. During a sesshin it is both an inspiration and a welcome relief. It also enables the practice to penetrate through to those more literal parts of our personality, those parts that are like a crust that has hardened through our abuse of the gift of language—the gift of the gods and the curse of Adam.

8

Answers to
Common Questions

You mentioned Soto and Rinzai. What is the difference between these two schools of Zen?

It is unfortunate that we in the West have inherited this opposition, which is essentially a Japanese problem. There is fundamentally no difference between these two Zen sects; there is just a question of emphasis. The Soto sect emphasizes the truth that we are already, as we are, here and now, fully awakened, whereas the Rinzai emphasizes the importance of knowing this existentially for ourselves. It is like the difference between someone who says, "The taste of ice cream is great," and someone else who tastes it and says, "Yes, it is."

But isn't the real difference that the Rinzai sect insists on awakening and the Soto says we do not need to come to awakening?

It is a mistake to believe that the Soto masters say we do not need to come to awakening. Dogen, the founder of the Japanese Soto sect, clearly came to awakening after hearing his teacher scold a sleepy monk. Tung-shan Liang-chieh, the founder of the Chinese equivalent of the Soto school, came to awakening upon seeing his reflection in a stream. If *they* came to awakening, why should they deny this to others?

I understand that in some Zen centers the discipline is very strict. If Zen is a way of liberation, isn't this a contradiction?

If one believes that submitting to discipline has any merit in itself, then you are right. However, if one recognizes that discipline is a means to an end, where is the contradiction? Our attention is normally so scattered that our first problem is to collect ourselves. This collecting ourselves we could call discipline. If the means to do this comes from within, then it is self-discipline; if from without, then it is discipline. It is interesting that, provided the discipline is related solely to this gathering ourselves together and not related to a power trip on the part of the teacher or a dependency trip on the part of the participant, the more exacting the discipline, the easier it is to work on oneself.

However, a danger can arise in that this freedom to work on oneself can be mistaken for true freedom, and conformity mistaken for spiritual advancement. If one is to submit to discipline, one must maintain a maverick outlook. In any case, no discipline should impinge upon one's autonomy or self-respect.

I still do not understand the point of ritual and worship in Zen. Isn't that a kind of conditioning?

This question cannot be answered satisfactorily in a few words. First of all, we must remember that there are different types of people, some of whom must be appealed to through the mind, others through the emotions, others through physical sensation, still others through symbols, and so on. Furthermore, ritual has nothing to do with conceptual thinking and cannot be explained conceptually. For example, if you wanted to get someone to know about the joy of swimming, what would you do? Surely get them into the water. Some things, perhaps most things, we can only know by doing. Finally, implicit in your question is the modern fear of conditioning. We are all terrified of being *conditioned*. Yet the answer to conditioning is not to resist conditioning, but to be mindful. The problem is that life is one long hypnotic session; the solution is to wake up.

Can one practice Zen while being a practicing Christian?

It depends upon whose Zen and whose Christianity. For example, consider the following quotes: "God dwells or is present substantially in every soul, even the soul of the greatest sinner. This kind of union is never lacking since it is in and by this union that He sustains their being." But there is another kind of union "which can only come about when the soul attains to a likeness with God by virtue of love." With very little effort one can take the first statement as reflecting the Soto view: that we are already awakened and that there is no need to come to union with God because union with God is our very nature. The second type of union corresponds to the Rinzai belief: one must come to awakening; union with God must be achieved.

These Christian quotations are from St. John of the Cross. I have often recommended him to people as a source of great inspiration. Meister Eckhart, another great Christian, says, "God makes us to know, and his knowing is his being, and his making me know is that same as my knowing, so his knowing is mine." Eckhart is here speaking about the clear knowing that we referred to earlier, which is as much the "other" knowing me as me knowing the "other." Both St. John and Meister Eckhart insist that the only way to union with God is through letting go of all images, thoughts, and forms of God, and, furthermore, that such union is not a new situation but the discovery of that which has been from the very beginning.

For such Christians, awakening is proof of God's infinite mercy; for the Zen Buddhist, union with God is seeing into our true nature. However, there are Christians for whom the important fact is the uniqueness of Christ as the only true manifestation of God-as-man. And there are Zen Buddhists for whom what matters is that practice should be carried on according to a strict model and that rituals should all be unequivocally Buddhist. For these Christians and Zen Buddhists there can be no rapprochement. But in either case it is unwise to try to bring about a merging of Christianity and Buddhism; what is needed is to explore the ground that is neither Christian nor Buddhist.

> We shall not cease from exploration,
> And the end of all our exploring
> Will be to arrive where we started
> And know the place for the first time.
> —T. S. Eliot, *Four Quartets*